VIETNAM

OTHER BOOKS BY MARY MC CARTHY

The Company She Keeps

The Oasis

Cast a Cold Eye

The Groves of Academe

A Charmed Life

Sights and Spectacles

Memories of a Catholic Girlhood

Venice Observed

The Stones of Florence

On the Contrary

The Group

Mary McCarthy

VIETNAM

HARCOURT, BRACE & WORLD, INC., NEW YORK

First edition
Library of Congress Catalog Card Number: 67-28041
Printed in the United States of America

To Jim

Contents

The Home Program

I confess that when I went to Vietnam early last February I was looking for material damaging to the American interest and that I found it, though often by accident or in the process of being briefed by an official. Finding it is no job; the Americans do not dissemble what they are up to. They do not seem to feel the need, except through verbiage; *e.g.*, napalm has become "Incinderjell," which makes it sound like Jello. And defoliants are referred to as weed-killers—something you use in your driveway. The resort to euphemism denotes, no doubt, a guilty conscience or—the same thing nowadays—a twinge in the public-relations nerve. Yet what is most surprising to a new arrival in Saigon is the general unawareness, almost innocence, of how what "we" are doing could look to an outsider.

At the airport in Bangkok, the war greeted the Air France passengers in the form of a strong smell of gasoline, which made us sniff as we breakfasted at a long table, like a delegation, with the Air France flag—our banner—planted in the middle. Outside, huge Esso tanks were visible behind lattice screens, where U.S. bombers, factory-new, were aligned as if in a salesroom. On the field itself, a few yards from our Boeing 707, U.S. cargo planes were warming up for take-off; U.S. helicopters flitted about among the swallows, while U.S. military trucks made deliveries. The openness of the thing was amazing (the fact that the U.S. was using Thailand as a base for bombing North Vietnam was not officially admitted at the time); you would have thought they would try to camouflage it, I said to a German correspondent, so that the tourists would not see. As the 707 flew on toward Saigon, the tourists, bound for Tokyo or Manila, were able to watch a South Vietnamese hillside burning while consuming a "cool drink" served by the hostess. From above, the bright flames looked like a summer forest fire; you could not believe that bombers had just left. At Saigon, the airfield was dense with military aircraft; in the "civil" side, where we landed, a passenger jetliner was loading G.I.'s for Rest and Recreation in Hawaii. The American presence was overpowering, and, although one had read about it and was aware, as they say, that there was a war on, the sight and sound of that massed American might, casually disposed on foreign soil, like a corporal having his shoes shined, took one's breath away. "They don't try to hide it!" I kept saying to myself, as though the display of naked power and muscle ought to have worn some cover of modesty. But within a few hours I had lost this sense of incredulous surprise, and, seeing the word, "hide," on a note pad in my hotel room the next morning, I no longer knew what I had meant by it (as when a fragment of a dream, written down on waking; becomes indecipherable) or why I should have been pained, as an American, by this high degree of visibility.

As we drove into downtown Saigon, through a traffic jam, I had the fresh shock of being in what looked like an American city, a very shoddy West Coast one, with a Chinatown and a slant-eyed Asiatic minority. Not only military vehicles of every description, but Chevrolets, Chryslers, Mercedes-Benz, Volkswagens, Triumphs, and white men everywhere in sport shirts and drip-dry pants. The civilian take-over is even more astonishing than the military. To an American, Saigon today is less exotic than Florence or the Place de la Concorde. New office buildings of cheap modern design, teeming with teazed, puffed secretaries and their Washington bosses, are surrounded by sandbags and guarded by M.P.'s; new, jerry-built villas in pastel tones, to rent to Americans, are under construction or already beginning to peel and discolor. Even removing the sandbags and the machine guns and restoring the trees that have been chopped down to widen the road to the airport, the mind cannot excavate what Saigon must have been like "before." Now it resembles a gigantic PX. All those white men seem to be carrying brown paper shopping bags, full of whiskey and other goodies; rows of ballpoints gleam in the breast pockets of their checked shirts. In front of his villa, a leathery oldster, in visored cap, unpacks his golf clubs from his station wagon, while his cotton-haired wife, in a flowered print dress, glasses slung round her neck, stands by, watching, her hands on her hips. As in the American vacation-land, dress is strictly informal; nobody but an Asian wears a tie or a white shirt. The Vietnamese old men and boys, in wide, conical hats, pedaling their Cyclos (the modern version of the rickshaw) in and out of the traffic pattern, the Vietnamese women in high heels and filmy ao-dais of pink, lavender, heliotrope, the signs and Welcome banners in Vietnamese actually contribute to the Stateside impression by the addition of "local" color, as though you were back in a Chinese restaurant in San Francisco or in a Japanese sukiyaki place, under swaying paper lanterns, being served by women in kimonos while you sit on mats and play at using chopsticks.

Perhaps most of all Saigon is like a stewing Los Angeles, shading into Hollywood, Venice Beach, and Watts. The native stall markets are still in business, along Le Loi and Nguyen Hue Streets, but the merchandise is, for Asia, exotic. There is hardly anything native to buy, except flowers and edibles and firecrackers at Têt time and—oh yes—souvenir dolls. Street vendors and children are offering trays of American cigarettes and racks on racks of Johnnie Walker, Haig & Haig, Black & White (which are either black market, stolen from the PX, or spurious, depending on the price); billboards outside car agencies advertise Triumphs, Thunderbirds, MG's, Corvettes, "For Delivery here or Stateside, Payment on Easy Terms"; non-whites, the less affluent ones, are mounted on Hondas and Lambrettas. There are photo-copying services, film-developing services, Western tailoring and dry-cleaning services, radio and TV repair shops, air conditioners, Olivetti typewriters, comic books, *Time, Life,* and *Newsweek,* airmail paper—you name it, they have it. Toys for Vietnamese children (there are practically no American kids or wives in Vietnam) include U.S.-style jackknives, pistols, and simulated-leather belts, with holsters—I did not see any cowboy suits or Indian war-feathers. Pharmaceuticals are booming; young Vietnamese women of the upper crust are enrolling in the School of Pharmacy in order to open drugstores; and a huge billboard all along the top of a building in the central marketplace shows a smiling Negro—maybe a long-ago Senegalese soldier—with very white teeth advertising a toothpaste called Hynos.

If Saigon by day is like a PX, at night, with flares overhead, it is like a World's Fair or Exposition in some hick American city.

There are Chinese restaurants, innumerable French restaurants (not surprising), but also La Dolce Vita, Le Guillaume Tell, the Paprika (a Spanish restaurant on a rooftop, serving paella and sangría). The national cuisine no American wants to sample is the Vietnamese. In February, a German circus was in town. "French" wine is made in Cholon, the local Chinatown. In the night clubs, if it were not for the bar girls, you would think you were on a cruise ship: a *chanteuse* from Singapore sings old French, Italian, and American favorites into the microphone; an Italian magician palms the watch of a middle-aged Vietnamese customer; the band strikes up "Happy Birthday to You," as a cake is brought in. The "vice" in Saigon—at least what I was able to observe of it—has a pepless *Playboy* flavor.

As for virtue, I went to church one Sunday in the Cathedral (a medley of Gothic, Romanesque, and vaguely Moorish) on John F. Kennedy Square, hoping to hear the mass in Vietnamese. Instead, an Irish-American priest preached a sermon on the hemline to a large male white congregation of soldiers, construction-workers, newspaper correspondents; in the pews were also a few female secretaries from the Embassy and other U.S. agencies and a quotient of middle-class Vietnamese of both sexes. I had happened, it turned out, on the "American" mass, said at noon. Earlier services *were* in Vietnamese. The married men present, the celebrant began, did not have to be told that the yearly rise or fall in skirt lengths was a "traumatic experience" for a woman, and he likened the contemporary style centers—New York, Chicago, San Francisco—to the ancient "style centers" of the Church—Rome, Antioch, Jerusalem. His point seemed to be that the various rites of the Church (Latin, Coptic,

Armenian, Maronite—he went into it very thoroughly) were only *modes* of worship. What the Sunday-dressed Vietnamese, whose hemline remains undisturbed by changes emanating from the "style centers" and who were hearing the Latin mass in American, were able to make of the sermon, it was impossible to tell. Just as it was impossible to tell what some very small Vietnamese children I saw in a home for ARVN war orphans were getting out of an American adult TV program they were watching at bedtime, the littlest ones mother-naked. Maybe TV, too, is catholic, and the words do not matter.

Saigon has a smog problem, like New York and Los Angeles, a municipal garbage problem, a traffic problem, power failures, inflation, juvenile delinquency. In short, it meets most of the criteria of a modern Western city. The young soldiers do not like Saigon and its clip joints and high prices. Everybody is trying to sell them something or buy something from them. Six-year-old boys, cute as pins, are plucking at them: "You come see my sister. She Number One fuck." To help the G.I. resist the temptations of merchants—and soak up his buying power—diamonds and minks are offered him in the PX, tax free. (There were no minks the day I went there, but I did see a case of diamond rings, the prices ranging up to 900-odd dollars.) Unfortunately, the PX presents its own temptation—that of resale. The G.I. is gypped by taxi drivers and warned against Cyclo men (probably VC), and he may wind up in a Vietnamese jail, like some of his buddies, for doing what everybody else does—illegal currency transactions. If he walks in the center after nightfall, he has to pick his way among whole families who are cooking their unsanitary meal or sleeping, right on the street, in the filth.

When he rides in from the airport, he has to cross a bend of the river, bordered by shanties, that he has named, with rich American humor, Cholera Creek.

To the servicemen, Saigon stinks. They would rather be in base camp, which is clean. And the JUSPAO press officer has a rote speech for arriving correspondents: "Get out of Saigon. That's my advice to you. Go out into the field." As though the air were purer there, where the fighting is.

That is true in a way. The Americanization process smells better out there, to Americans, even when perfumed by napalm. Out there, too, there is an enemy a man can respect. For many of the soldiers in the field and especially the younger officers, the Viet Cong is the only Vietnamese worthy of notice. "If we only had them fighting on our side, instead of the goddamned Arvin [Army of the Vietnamese Republic], we'd *win* this war" is a sentiment the newspapermen like to quote. I never heard it said in those words, but I found that you could judge an American by his attitude toward the Viet Cong. If he called them "Charlie" (*cf.* John Steinbeck), he was either an infatuated civilian, a low-grade primitive in uniform, or a fatuous military mouthpiece. Decent soldiers and officers called them "the VC." The same code of honor applied in South Vietnamese circles; with the Vietnamese, who are ironic, it was almost a pet name for the enemy. Most of the American military will praise the fighting qualities of the VC, and the more intellectual (who are not necessarily the best) praise them for their "motivation." In this half of the century Americans have become very incurious, but the Viet Cong has awakened the curiosity of the men who are fighting them. From within the perimeter of the camp, behind the barbed wire and the sandbags, they study their habits, half-amused, half-admiring; a gingerly relationship is established with the unseen enemy, who is probably carefully fashioning a booby trap a few hundred yards away. This relation does not seem to extend to the North Vietnamese troops, but in that case contact is rarer. The military are justly nervous of the VC, but unless they have been wounded out on a patrol or have had the next man killed by a mine or a mortar, they do not show hatred or picture the black-pajama saboteur as a "monster," a word heard in Saigon offices.

In the field, moreover, the war is not questioned; it is just a fact. The job has to be finished—that is the attitude. In Saigon, the idea that the war can ever be finished appears fantastic: the Americans will be there forever, one feels; if they go, the economy will collapse. What postwar aid program could be conceived—or passed by Congress—that would keep the air in the balloon? And if the Americans go, the middle-class Saigonese think, the Viet Cong will surely come back, in two years, five years, ten, as they come back to a "pacified" hamlet at Têt time, to leave, as it were, a calling card, a reminder—we are still here. But, at the same time, in Saigon the worth of the American presence, that is, of the war, seems very dubious, since the actual results, in uglification, moral and physical, are evident to all. The American soldier, bumping along in a jeep or a military truck, resents seeing all those Asiatics at the wheels of new Cadillacs. He knows about corruption, often firsthand, having contributed his bit to it, graft, theft of AID and military supplies from the port. He thinks it is disgusting that the local employees steal from the PX and then stage a strike when the manageress makes them line up to be searched on leaving the building. And he has heard that these "apes," as some men call them, are salting away the profits in Switzerland or in France, where De Gaulle, who is pro-VC, has just run the army out.

Of course, all wars have had their profiteers, but it has not usually been so manifest, so inescapable. The absence of the austerity that normally accompanies war, of civilian sacrifices, rationing, shortages, blackouts (compare wartime London or even wartime New York, twenty-five years ago) makes this war seem singularly immoral and unheroic to those who are likely to die in it—for what? So that the Saigonese and other civilians can live high off the hog? The fact that the soldier or officer is living pretty high off the hog himself does not reconcile him to the glut of Saigon; rather the contrary. Furthermore, an atmosphere of sacrifice is heady; that—and danger—is what used to make wartime capitals gay. Saigon is not gay. The peculiar thing is that with all those young soldiers wandering about, all those young journalists news-chasing, Saigon seems so middle-aged—inert, listless, bored. That, I suppose, is because everyone's principal interest there is money, the only currency that is circulating, like the stale air moved by ceiling fans and air conditioners in hotels and offices.

The war, they say, is not going to be won in Saigon, nor on the battlefield, but in the villages and hamlets. This idea, by now trite (it was first discovered in Diem's time and has been rebaptized under a number of names—New Life Hamlets, Rural Construction, Counter Insurgency, Nation-Building, Revolutionary Development, the Hearts and Minds Program), is the main source of inspiration for the various teams of missionaries, military and civilian, who think they are engaged in a crusade. Not just a crusade against Communism, but something *positive*. Back in the fifties and early sixties, the war was presented as an investment: the taxpayer was persuaded that if he stopped Communism *now* in Vietnam, he would not have to keep stopping it in Thailand, Burma, etc. That was the domino theory, which our leading statesmen today, quite comically, are busy repudiating before Congressional committees—suddenly nobody will admit to ever having been an advocate of it. The notion of a costly investment that will save money in the end has a natural appeal to a nation of homeowners, but now the assertion of an American "interest" in Vietnam has begun to look too speculative as the stake increases ("When is it going to pay off?") and also too squalid as the war daily becomes more savage and destructive. Hence the "other" war, proclaimed by President Johnson in Honolulu, which is simultaneously pictured as a strategy for winning War Number One and as a top priority in itself. Indeed, in Vietnam, there are moments when the "other" war seems to be viewed as the sole reason for the American presence, and it is certainly more congenial to American officials, brimming with public spirit, than the war they are launching from the skies. Americans do not like to be negative, and the "other" war is constructive.

To see it, of course, you have to get out of Saigon, but, before you go, you will have to be briefed, in one of those new office buildings, on what you are going to see. In the field, you will be briefed again, by a military man, in a district or province headquarters, and frequently all you will see of New Life Hamlets, Constructed Hamlets, Consolidated Hamlets are the charts and graphs and maps and symbols that some ardent colonel or brisk bureaucrat is demonstrating to you with a pointer, and the mimeographed handout, full of statistics, that you take away with you, together with a supplement on Viet Cong Terror. On paper and in chart form, it all sounds commendable, especially if you are able to ignore the sounds of bombing from B-52's that are shaking the windows and making the charts rattle. The briefing official is enthusiastic, as he points out the progress that has been made, when, for example, the activities organized under AID were reorganized under OCO (Office of Civilian Operations). You stare at the chart on the office wall in which to you there is no semblance of logic or sequence ("Why," you wonder, "should Youth Affairs be grouped under Urban Development?"), and the official rubs his hands with pleasure: "First we organized it *vertically*. Now we've organized it *horizontally!*" He does not say that one of the main reasons for the creation of OCO was to provide a cover for certain CIA activities. Out in the field, you learn from some disgruntled officer that the AID representatives, who are perhaps now OCO representatives without knowing it, have not been paid for six months.

In a Saigon "backgrounder," you are told about public-health measures undertaken by Free World Forces. Again a glowing progress report. In 1965, there were 180 medical people from the "Free World" in Vietnam treating patients; in 1966, there were 700—quite a little escalation, almost four times as many. The troop commitment, of course, not mentioned by the briefer, jumped from 60,000 to 400,000—more than six-and-a-half times as many. That the multiplication of troops implied an obvious escalation in the number of civilian patients requiring treatment is not mentioned either. Under questioning, the official, slightly irritated, estimates that the civilian casualties comprise between 7½ and 15 per cent of the surgical patients treated in hospitals. He had "not been interested particularly, until all the furore," in what percentage of the patients were war casualties. And naturally he was not interested in what percentage of civilian casualties never reached a hospital at all.

Nor would there have been any point in asking him what happens to the Viet Cong wounded—a troubling question I never heard raised in nearly a month in Vietnam. A very few are in hospitals—some have been seen recently by a journalist in Can Tho—and the mother of a Marine killed in action has made public in a Texas newspaper a letter from her boy telling how he felt when ordered to go back to the battlefield and shoot wounded VC in the head (prompt denial from the Marine Corps). But American officials on the spot are not concerned by the discrepancy between estimated VC wounded and estimated VC in hospitals: 225 being treated in U.S. medical facilities in one week in May, whereas at the end of April an estimated 30,000 to 35,000 had been wounded in action since the first of the year.

But—to return to the "backgrounder"—the treatment of war victims, it turned out, was not one of the medical "bull's-eyes" aimed at in the "other" war. Rather, a peacetime-type program, "beefing up" the medical school, improvement of hospital facilities, donation of drugs and antibiotics (which, as I learned from another source, are in turn *sold* by the local nurses to the patients for whom they have been prescribed), the control of epidemic diseases, such as plague and cholera, education of the population in good health procedures. American and allied workers, you hear, are teaching the Vietnamese in the government villages to boil their water, and the children are learning dental hygiene. Toothbrushes are distributed, and the children are shown how to use them. If the children get the habit, the parents will copy them, a former social worker explains, projecting from experience with first-generation immigrants back home. There is a campaign on to vaccinate and immunize as much of the population as can be got to co-operate; easy subjects are refugees and forced évacués, who can be lined up for shots while going through the screening process and being issued an identity card—a political health certificate.

All this is not simply on paper. In the field, you are actually able to see medical teams at work, setting up temporary dispensaries under the trees in the hamlets for the weekly or biweekly "sick call"—distributing medicines, tapping, listening, sterilizing, bandaging; the most common diagnosis is suspected tuberculosis. In Tay Ninh Province, I watched a Philcag (Filipino) medical team at work in a Buddhist hamlet. One doctor was examining a very thin old man, who was stripped to the waist; probably tubercular, the doctor told me, writing something on a card which he gave to the old man. "What happens next?" I wanted to know. Well, the old man would go to the province hospital for an X ray (that was the purpose of the card), and if the diagnosis was positive, then treatment should follow. I was impressed. But (as I later learned at a briefing) there are only sixty civilian hospitals in South Vietnam—for nearly 16 million people—so that the old man's total benefit, most likely, from the open-air consultation was to have learned, gratis, that he might be tubercular.

Across the road, some dentist's chairs were set up, and teeth were being pulled, very efficiently, from women and children of all ages. I asked about the toothbrushes I had heard about in Saigon. The Filipino major laughed. "Yes, we have distributed them. They use them as toys." Then he reached into his pocket—he was a kindly young man with children of his own—and took out some money for all the children who had gathered round to buy popsicles (the local equivalent) from the popsicle man. Later I watched the Filipino general, a very handsome tall man with a cropped head, resembling Yul Brynner, distribute Têt gifts and candy to children in a Cao Dai orphanage and be photographed with his arm around a little blind girl. A few hours earlier, he had posed distributing food in a Catholic hamlet—"Free World" surplus items, such as canned cooked beets. The photography, I was told, would help sell the Philcag operation to the Assembly in Manila, where some leftist elements were trying to block funds for it. Actually, I could not see that the general was doing any harm, whatever his purposes might be, politically—unless not doing more is harm, in which case we are all guilty—and he was more efficient than other Civic Action leaders. His troops had just chopped down a large section of jungle (we proceeded through it in convoy, wearing bulletproof vests and bristling with rifles and machine guns, because of the VC), which was going to be turned into a hamlet for resettling refugees. They had also built a school, which we stopped to inspect, finding, to the general's surprise, that it had been taken over by the local district chief for his office headquarters.

The Filipino team, possibly because they were Asians, seemed to be on quite good terms with the population. Elsewhere—at Go Cong, in the delta—I saw mistrustful patients and heard stories of rivalry between the Vietnamese doctor, a gynecologist, and the Spanish and American medical teams; my companion and I were told that we were the first "outsiders," including the resident doctors, to be allowed by the Vietnamese into *his* wing—the maternity, which was far the cleanest and most modern in the hospital and contained one patient. Similar jealousies existed of the German medical staff at Hue. In the rather squalid surgical wing of the Go Cong hospital, there were two badly burned children. Were they war casualties, I asked the official who was showing us through. Yes, he conceded, as a matter of fact they were. How many of the patients were war-wounded, I wanted to know. "About four" of the children, he reckoned. And one old man, he added, after reflection.

The Filipinos were fairly dispassionate about their role in pacification; this may have been because they had no troops fighting in the war (those leftist elements in the Assembly!) and therefore did not have to act like saviors of the Vietnamese people. The Americans, on the contrary, are zealots—above all, the blueprinters in the Saigon offices—although occasionally in the field, too, you meet a true believer—a sandy, crew-cut, keen-eyed army colonel who talks to you about "the nuts and bolts" of the program, which, he is glad to say, is finally getting the "grass roots" support it needs. It is impossible to find out from such a man what he is doing, concretely; an aide steps forward to state, "We sterilize the area prior to the insertion of the RD teams," whose task, says the colonel, is to find out "the aspirations of the people." He cannot tell you whether there has been any land reform in his area—that is a strictly Vietnamese pigeon—in fact he has no idea of *how* the land in the area is owned. He is strong on co-ordination: all his Vietnamese counterparts, the colonel who "wears two hats" as province chief, the mayor, a deposed general, are "very fine sound men," and the Marine general in the area is "one of the finest men and officers" he has ever met. For another army zealot every Vietnamese officer he deals with is "an outstanding individual."

These springy, zesty, burning-eyed warriors, military and civilian, engaged in AID or Combined Action (essentially pacification) stir faraway memories of American college presidents of the fund-raising type; their diction is peppery with oxymoron ("When peace breaks out," "Then the commodities started to hit the beach"), like a college president's address to an alumni dinner. They see themselves in fact as educators, spreading the American way of life, a new *propaganda fide*. When I asked an OCO man in Saigon what his groups actually did in a Vietnamese village to prepare—his word—the people for elections, he answered curtly, "We teach them Civics 101."

The American taxpayer who thinks that aid means help has missed the idea. Aid is, first of all, to achieve economic stability within the present system, *i.e.*, political stability for the present ruling groups. Loans are extended, under the counterpart-fund arrangement, to finance Vietnamese imports of American capital equipment (thus AIDing, with the other hand, American industry). Second, aid is *education.* Distribution of canned goods (instill new food habits), distribution of seeds, fertilizer, chewing gum and candy (the Vietnamese complain that the G.I.'s fire candy at their children, like a spray of bullets), lessons in sanitation, hog-raising, and crop rotation. The program is designed, not just to make Americans popular, but to shake up the Vietnamese, as in some "stimulating" freshman course where the student learns to question the "prejudices" implanted in him by his parents. "We're trying to wean them away from the old barter economy and show them a market economy. Then they'll really *go.*"

"We're teaching them free enterprise," explains a breathless JUSPAO official in the grim town of Phu Cuong. He is speaking of the "refugees" from the Iron Triangle, who were forcibly cleared out of their hamlets, which were then burned and leveled, during Operation Cedar Falls ("Clear and Destroy"). They had just been transferred into a camp, hastily constructed by the ARVN with tin roofs painted red and white, to make the form, as seen from the air, of a giant Red Cross—1,651 women, 3,754 children, 582 men, mostly old, who had been kindly allowed to bring some of their furniture and pots and pans and their pigs and chickens and sacks of their hoarded rice; their water cattle had been transported for them, on barges, and were now sickening on a dry, stubbly, sandy plain. "We've got a captive audience!" the official continued excitedly. "This is our big chance!"

To teach them free enterprise and, presumably, when they were "ready" for it, Civics 101; for the present, the government had to consider them "hostile civilians." These wives and children and old fathers of men thought to be at large with the Viet Cong had been rice farmers only a few weeks before. Now they were going to have to pitch in and learn to be vegetable farmers; the area selected for their eventual resettlement was not suitable for rice-growing, unfortunately. Opportunity was beckoning for these poor peasants, thanks to the uprooting process they had just undergone. They would have the chance to buy and build their own homes on a pattern and of materials already picked out for them; the government was allowing them 1,700 piasters toward the purchase price. To get a new house free, even though that would seem only fair in the abstract, would be unfair to them as human beings, it was explained to me: investing their own labor and their own money would make them feel that the house was really *theirs*. "The Lord helps those who help themselves"—the social worker's Great Commandment—is interpreted in war-pounded Vietnam, and with relentless priggery, as "the U.S. helps those who help themselves."

In the camp, a schoolroom had been set up. Interviews with the parents revealed that more than anything else they wanted education for their children; they had not had a school for five years. I remarked that this seemed queer, since Communists were usually strong on education. The official insisted. "Not for five years." But in fact another American, a young one, who had actually been working in the camp, told me that strangely enough the small children there knew their multiplication tables and possibly their primer—he could not account for this. And in one of the razed villages, he related, the Americans had found, from captured exercise books, that someone had been teaching the past participle in English, using Latin models—defectors spoke of a high-school teacher, a Ph.D. from Hanoi.

Perhaps the parents, in the interviews, told the Americans what they thought they wanted to hear. All over Vietnam, wherever peace has broken out, if only in the form of a respite, Marine and army officers are proud to show the schoolhouses their men are building or rebuilding for the hamlets they are patrolling, rifle on shoulder. At Rach Kien, in the delta (a Pentagon pilot project of a few months before), I saw the little schoolhouse Steinbeck wrote about, back in January, and the blue school desks he had seen the soldiers painting. They were still sitting outside, in the sun; the school was not yet rebuilt more than a month later—they were waiting for materials. In this hamlet, everything seemed to have halted, as in "The Sleeping Beauty," the enchanted day Steinbeck left; nothing had advanced. Indeed, the picture he sketched, of a ghost town coming back to civic life, made the officers who had entertained him smile—"He used his imagination." In other hamlets, I saw schoolhouses actually finished and one in operation. "The school is dirty," the colonel in charge barked at the alarmed Revolutionary Development director, who claimed to have been the first to translate Pearl Buck into Vietnamese. It was an instance of American tactlessness, though the belligerent colonel was right. A young Vietnamese social worker said sadly that he wished the Americans would stop building schools. "They don't realize—we have no teachers for them."

Yet the little cream schoolhouse is essential to the American dream of what we are doing in Vietnam, and it is essential for the soldiers to believe that in *Viet Cong* hamlets no schooling is permitted. In Rach Kien I again expressed doubts, as a captain, with a professionally shocked face, pointed out the evidence that the school had been used as "Charlie's" headquarters. "So you really think that the children here got no lessons, *nothing*, under the VC?" "Oh, indoctrination courses!" he answered with a savvy wave of his pipe. In other words, VC Civics 101.

If you ask a junior officer what he thinks our war aims are in Vietnam, he usually replies without hesitation: "To punish aggression." It is unkind to try to draw him into a discussion of what constitutes aggression and what is defense (the Bay of Pigs, Santo Domingo, Goa?), for he really has no further ideas on the subject. He has been indoctrinated, just as much as the North Vietnamese P.O.W., who tells the interrogation team he is fighting to "liberate the native soil from the American aggressors"—maybe more. Only, the young American does not know it; he probably imagines that he is *thinking* when he produces that formula. And yet he does believe in something profoundly, though he may not be able to find the words for it: free enterprise. A parcel that to the American mind wraps up for delivery hospitals, sanitation, roads, harbors, schools, air travel, Jack Daniel's, convertibles, Stimudents. That is the C-ration that keeps him going. The American troops are not exactly conscious of bombing, shelling, and defoliating to defend free enterprise (which they cannot imagine as being under serious attack), but they plan to come out of the war with their values intact. Which means that they must spread them, until everyone is convinced, by demonstration, that the American way is better, just as American seed strains are better and American pigs are better. Their conviction is sometimes baldly stated. North of Da Nang, at a

Marine base, there is an ice-cream plant on which is printed in large official letters the words: "ICE-CREAM PLANT: ARVN MORALE BUILDER." Or it may wear a humanitarian disguise, *e.g.*, Operation Concern, in which a proud little town in Kansas airlifted 110 pregnant sows to a humble little town in Vietnam.

Occasionally the profit motive is undisguised. Flying to Hue in a big C-130, I heard the pilot and the co-pilot discussing their personal war aim, which was to make a killing, as soon as the war was over, in Vietnamese real estate. From the air, while they kept an eye out for VC, they had surveyed the possibilities and had decided on Nha Trang—"beautiful sand beaches"—better than Cam Ranh Bay—a "desert." They disagreed as to the kind of development that would make the most money: the pilot wanted to build a high-class hotel and villas, while the co-pilot thought that the future lay with low-cost housing. I found this conversation hallucinating, but the next day, in Hue, I met a Marine colonel who was back in uniform after retirement; having fought the Japanese, he had made his killing as a "developer" in Okinawa and invested the profits in a frozen-shrimp import business (from Japan) supplying restaurants in San Diego. War, a cheap form of mass tourism, opens the mind to business opportunities.

All these developers were Californians. In fact, the majority of the Americans I met in the field in Vietnam were WASPs from Southern California; most of the rest were from the rural South. In nearly a month I met *one* Jewish boy in the services (a nice young naval officer from Pittsburgh), two Boston Irish, and a captain from Connecticut. Given the demographic shift toward the Pacific in the United States, this Californian ascendancy gave me the peculiar feeling that I was seeing the future of our country as if on a movie screen. Nobody has dared make a war movie about Vietnam, but the prevailing unreality, as experienced in base camps and headquarters, is eerily like a movie, a contest between good and evil, which is heading toward a happy ending, when men with names like "Colonel Culpepper," "Colonel Derryberry," "Captain Stanhope" will vanquish Victor Charlie. The state that has a movie actor for governor and a movie actor for U.S. senator seemed to be running the show.

No doubt the very extensive press and television coverage of the war has made the participants very conscious of "exposure," that is, of role-playing. Aside from the usual networks, Italian television, Mexican television, the BBC, CBC were all filming the "other" war during the month of February, and the former Italian Chief of Staff, General Liuzzi, was covering it as a commentator for the *Corriere della Sera.* The effect of all this attention on the generals, colonels, and lesser officers was to put a premium on "sincerity."

Nobody likes to be a villain, least of all a WASP officer, who feels he is playing the heavy in Vietnam through some awful mistake in typecasting. He *knows* he is good at heart, because everything in his home environment—his TV set, his paper, his Frigidaire, the President of the United States—has promised him that, whatever shortcomings he may have as an individual, collectively he is good. The "other" war is giving him the chance to clear up the momentary misunderstanding created by those bombs, which, through no fault of his, are happening to hit civilians. He has *warned* them to get away, dropped leaflets saying he was coming and urging "Charlie" to defect, to join the other side; lately, in pacified areas, he has even taken the precaution of having his targets cleared by the village chief before shelling or bombing, so that now the press officer giving the daily briefing is able to reel out: "Operation Blockhouse. 29 civilians reported wounded today. Two are in 'poor' condition. Target had been approved by the district chief." Small thanks he gets, our military hero, for that scrupulous restraint. But in the work of pacification, his real self comes out, clear and true. Digging wells for the natives (too bad if the water comes up brackish), repairing roads ("Just a jungle trail before we came," says the captain, though his colonel, in another part of the forest, has just been saying that the engineers had uncovered a fine stone roadbed built eighty years ago by the French), building a house for the widow of a Viet Cong (so far unreconciled; it takes time).

American officers in the field can become very sentimental when they think of the good they are doing and the hard row they have to hoe with the natives, who have been brainwashed by the Viet Cong. A Marine general in charge of logistics in I-Corps district was deeply moved when he spoke of his Marines: moving in to help rebuild some refugee housing with scrap lumber and sheet tin (the normal materials were cardboard boxes and flattened beer cans); working in their off-hours to build desks for a school; giving their Christmas money for a new high school; planning a new marketplace. The Marine Corps had donated a children's hospital, and in that hospital, right up the road ("Your ve-hickels will conduct you"—he pronounced it like "nickels") was a little girl who had been wounded during a Marine assault. "We're nursing her back to health," he intoned—and paused, like a preacher accustomed, at this point, to hearing an "Amen"; his PIO (Information Officer) nodded three times. In the hospital, I asked to see the little girl. "Oh, she's gone home," said the PIO. "Nursed her back to health." In reality the little girl was still there, but it was true, her wounds were nearly healed.

A young Marine doctor, blue-eyed, very good-looking, went from bed to bed, pointing out what was the matter with each child and showing what was being done to cure it. There was only the one war casualty; the rest were suffering from malnutrition (the basic complaint everywhere), skin diseases, worms; one had a serious heart condition; two had been badly burned by a stove, and one, in the contagious section, had the plague. The doctor showed us the tapeworm, in a bottle, he had extracted from one infant. A rickety baby was crying, and a middle-aged corpsman picked it up and gave it its bottle. They were plainly doing a good job, under makeshift conditions and without laboratory facilities. The children who were well enough to sit up appeared content; some even laughed, shyly. No amusements were provided for them, but perhaps it was sufficient amusement to be visited by tiptoeing journalists. And it could not be denied that it was a break for these children to be in a Marine hospital, clean, well-fed, and one to a bed. They were benefiting from the war, at least for the duration of their stay; the doctor was not sanguine, for the malnutrition cases, about what would happen when the patients went home. "We keep them as long as we can," he said, frowning. "But we can't keep them forever. They have to go back to their parents."

Compared to what they were used to, this short taste of the American way of life no doubt was delicious for Vietnamese children. John Morgan, in the London *Sunday Times,* described another little Vietnamese girl up near the DMZ—do they have one to a battalion?—who had been wounded by Marine bullets ("A casualty of war," that general repeated solemnly. "A casualty of war") and whom he saw carried in one night to a drinking party in sick bay, her legs bandaged, a spotlight playing on her, while the Marines pressed candy and dollar bills into her hands and had their pictures taken with her; she had more dolls than Macy's, they told him—"that girl is real spoiled." To spoil a child you have injured and send her back to her parents, with her dolls as souvenirs, is pharisee virtue, just as it is pharisaical to fill a child's stomach and send it home to be hungry again. The young doctor, being a doctor, was possibly conscious of the fakery—from a responsible medical point of view—of the "miracle" cures he was effecting; that was why he frowned. Meanwhile, however, the Marine Corps brass could show the "Before" and "After" to a captive audience. In fact two. The studio audience of children, smiling and laughing and clapping, and the broader audience of their parents, who, when allowed to visit, could not fail to be awed by the "other" side of American technology. And beyond that still a third audience—the journalists and their readers back home, who would recognize the Man in White and his corpsmen, having brought them up, gone to school with them, seen them on TV, in soap opera. I felt this myself, a relieved recognition of the familiar face of America. These are the American boys we know at once, even in an Asian context, bubbling an Asian baby. We do not recognize them, helmeted, in a bomber aiming cans of napalm at a thatched village. We have a credibility gap.

Leaving the hospital, I jolted southward in a jeep, hanging on, swallowing dust; the roads, like practically everything in Vietnam, have been battered, gouged, scarred, torn up by the weight of U.S. matériel. We passed Marines' laundry, yards and yards of it, hanging outside native huts—the dark-green battle cloth spelled money. Down the road was a refugee camp, which did not form part of the itinerary. This, I realized, must be "home" to some of the children we had just seen; the government daily allowance for a camp family was ten piasters (six cents) a day—sometimes twenty if there were two adults in the family. Somebody had put a streamer, in English, over the entrance: "REFUGEES FROM COMMUNISM."

This was a bit too much. The children's hospital had told the story the Americans were anxious to get over. Why put in the commercial? And who was the hard sell aimed at? Not the refugees, who could not read English and who, if they were like all the other refugees, had fled, some from the Viet Cong and some from the Americans and some because their houses had been bombed or shelled. Not the journalists, who knew better. Whoever carefully lettered that streamer, crafty Marine or civilian, had applied all his animal cunning to selling himself.

The Problems of Success

A short trip by helicopter from Saigon in almost any direction permits a ringside view of American bombing. Just beyond the truck gardens of the suburbs, you see what at first glance appears to be a series of bonfires evocative of Indian summers; thick plumes of smoke are rising from wooded clumps and fields. Toward the west, great blackish-brown tracts testify to the most recent results of the defoliation program; purplish-brown tracts are last year's work. As the helicopter skims the treetops, and its machine guns lower into position, you can study the fires more closely, and it is possible to distinguish a rice field burned over by peasants from neat bombing targets emitting spirals of smoke. But a new visitor cannot be sure and may tend to discredit his horrified impression, not wishing to jump to conclusions. Flying over the delta one morning, I saw the accustomed lazy smoke puffs mounting from the landscape and was urging myself to be cautious ("How do you *know?*") when I noticed a small plane circling; then it plunged, dropped its bombs, and was away in a graceful movement, having hit the target again; there was a flash of flame, and fresh, blacker smoke poured out. In the distance, a pair of small planes was hovering in the sky, like mosquitoes buzzing near the ceiling, waiting to strike. We flew on.

Coming back to Saigon in the afternoon, I expected to hear about "my" double air strike in the daily five o'clock press briefing, but no air activity in the sector was mentioned—too trivial to record, said a newsman. On a day taken at random (Washington's Birthday), the Air Force and the Marine Corps reported 460 sorties flown over *South* Vietnam "in support of ground forces"; whenever a unit is in trouble, they send for the airmen. Quite apart from the main battle areas, where fires and secondary explosions are announced as so many "scores," the countryside is routinely dotted with fires in various stages, so that they come to seem a natural part of it, like the grave mounds in the rice fields and pastures. The charred patches you see when returning in the afternoon from a morning's field trip are this morning's smoking embers; meanwhile, new curls of smoke, looking almost peaceful, are the afternoon's tally. And the cruel couples of hovering aircraft (they seem to travel in pairs, like FBI agents) appear to be daytime fixtures, almost stationary in the sky.

The Saigonese themselves are unaware of the magnitude of what is happening to their country, since they are unable to use military transport to get an aerial view of it; they only note the refugees sleeping in the streets and hear the B-52's pounding a few miles away. Seeing the war from the air, amid the crisscrossing Skyraiders, Supersabres, Phantoms, observation planes, Psywar planes (dropping leaflets), you ask yourself how much longer the Viet Cong can hold out; the country is so small that at the present rate of destruction there will be no place left for them to hide, not even under water, breathing through a straw. The plane and helicopter crews are alert for the slightest sign of movement in the fields and woods and estuaries below; they lean forward intently, scanning the ground. At night, the Dragon-ships come out, dropping flares and firing mini-guns.

The Air Force seems inescapable, like the Eye of God, and soon, you imagine (let us hope with hyperbole), all will be razed, charred, defoliated by that terrible searching gaze. Punishment can be magistral. A correspondent, who was tickled by the incident, described flying with the pilot of the little FAC plane that directs a big bombing mission; below, a lone Vietnamese on a bicycle stopped, looked up, dismounted, took up a rifle and fired; the pilot let him have it with the whole bombload of napalm—enough for a platoon. In such circumstances, anyone with a normal sense of fair play cannot help pulling for the bicyclist, but the sense of fair play, supposed to be Anglo-Saxon, has atrophied in the Americans here from lack of exercise. We draw a long face over Viet Cong "terror," but no one stops to remember that the Viet Cong does not possess that superior instrument of terror, an air force, which in our case, over South Vietnam at least, is acting almost with impunity. The worst thing that could happen to our country would be to win this war.

At the end of February, President Johnson's personal representative announced to the assembled press corps in Saigon that whereas ten months ago the U.S. had confronted "the prommlms of failure" (read "problems of failure") in Vietnam, now it confronted "the prommlms engendered by success." This Madison Avenue Mercury, once a CIA agent, whose lips flexed as he spoke like rubber bands, was concluding a whirlwind tour of the country, and he kept conspicuously raising his arm to study his wrist watch and frown during his brief appearance; in an hour or so he would be airborne to Washington, on a breeze of confidence. One of "the problems of success" he listed was the refugees. This swift conversion of a liability into an asset is typical of the current American approach to Vietnam.

It is true that the French, who failed, did not have the problem. As a blunt Marine colonel said in his battery headquarters: "We created the refugees. There weren't any in the French war. Everybody fought and then went home at night." Today all that has been changed. Early in February an OCO man estimated that 10 per cent of the population are now refugees—a million and a half, he reckoned, since January 1964. With every new American operation the figure of course is revised upward. Yet the technology that is able to generate a record production of homeless persons, surpassing the old norms reached by floods and earthquakes, is able to reverse itself, when a real emergency looms, and use its skills for a salvage or mercy operation in the manner of the Red Cross. The emergency occurred in January with the Iron Triangle victims, originally counted as about 8,000 civilians, who have been finally boiled down to the 5,987 persons in the camp at Phu Cuong.

These people, obviously, are not refugees at all in the dictionary sense of the word ("A person who flees his home or country to seek refuge elsewhere, as in time of war, political or religious persecution, etc."). They did not flee from the B-52's, though they might well have; they were moved by U.S. troops, who were systematically setting fire to their houses. Thanks to world press and television coverage, nobody could claim that they had "voted with their feet" to join the Free World. They did not use their feet; they were packed into army trucks and loaded onto boats. And here begins the story of how with nerve and enterprise you can convert a liability into an asset, not just by word manipulation, but by the kind of action that talks. The Americans moved in squarely to meet unfavorable publicity with favorable publicity. They changed their image, like so many vaudeville artists making a rapid costume change in the wings.

Let me be fair. No doubt humane considerations played a part in the decision to treat this particular group of "refugees" with kid gloves. Surely individuals in the Army were shocked and even sickened by the orders for Operation Cedar Falls coming from "higher up." Possibly Johnson's advisers sincerely regretted what was seen as a military necessity in terms of "shortening the war," "saving American lives," or whatever formula was applied. Anyway, Washington decided to do right by the "refugees."

It is paying off. The camp at Phu Cuong has become a showcase. Newspaper people and other visitors are flown in by military helicopter—a short run from Saigon—to see for themselves. Everything there is open and above board, contrary to what a suspicious person might think. You can interview the évacués through the camp interpreter if you have a mind to. Or you can bring your own interpreter and talk to them alone. Fresh water is brought in daily by army trucks and pumped steadily into reserve tanks. When I arrived, the pump had stopped working, but a colonel of Engineers was there in a trice to fix it, scratching his sandy head and using his American know-how. "These people are river people; they waste a lot of water," said the young camp supervisor. Latrines of a primitive kind had been built. The authorities were trying to teach the people not to squat behind their huts, to collect their garbage at the indicated pickup points instead of throwing it on the paths, not to splash water when ladling it out of the tank. Instructions in Vietnamese were plainly posted.

At noon, a Revolutionary Development cadre, in black pajamas, was supervising the rice distribution. The free market had been introduced—a novelty, it was said, to these peasant women and old peasant men. Merchants from the town came to sell fresh vegetables and buy canned and packaged products accumulated by the camp inhabitants, who received a daily ration as well as welfare payments and cash for what labor they did. In the beginning, the merchants had cheated the camp people, who did not know the fair market price of American surplus products, but the Americans had quickly put a stop to that. The évacués were learning to make bricks out of mud, water, and a little cement for the supports of their future homes, using an American moulding process called Cinvaram—all over Vietnam, wherever the Americans were "pacifying," there was Cinvaram, a singularly ugly gray brick. Six TV sets had been donated by AID; in time, the authorities hoped to get cleaner programs—striptease shows from Saigon were "kind of shocking" for backward peasant families with little kids. And in accordance with the Friendly Forces policy, the ARVN was getting a credit line for putting the camp on its feet; it was they who had done all the construction work, the Americans insisted—they themselves had only advised, supplied some materials, and the daily water delivery.

Any impartial person would concede that conditions were not too bad here, given the inevitable crowding. The "refugees" complained of the heat; in their river villages, there had been shade, and here there was not a tree, just an expanse of baking dust, which was regularly kicked up by arriving helicopters and military vehicles. They complained that their cattle were sick, that some of their hoarded rice had been stolen from them; not true, said the advisers: they had been *told* to mark it carefully and they had only themselves to blame if the unmarked sacks got mixed up in transit. They complained of the arrogance of the Revolutionary Development cadres, who were there to supervise them, one weedy youth to each group hut, and of the fact that spies had been placed among them; an indispensable measure, said the advisers, to prevent agitation and propaganda: after all, these people were Viet Cong dependents, and some troublemakers in their midst were trying to stir up a protest strike, playing on their little grievances. A number of the troublemakers were known to the authorities and would be dealt with; in time, the rest would be picked out.

But the young camp supervisor, a Quaker, was pleased on the whole with how things were going. One hundred and fifty families out of the original camp population had already agreed to go and learn to be rubber workers on a plantation, which had somewhat alleviated the crowding, and some new shelters were being built. To his mild astonishment, the camp had just been "passed" by the World Health Organization. He was keeping his fingers crossed about the strike, which, if it happened, would do the camp no good. The cadres identified as "arrogant" would soon be replaced, he hoped. Women whose husbands were Hoi

Chanh (defectors) in the nearby Chieu Hoi camp would eventually be allowed to join them, so that families would be reunited and resettled. It would be great when the school reopened, after the Têt holiday; the kids had already had one day of classes. As he passed, some of the bolder children touched him and ran away, laughing; he was popular. It was only when a military helicopter landed, I noticed, that the pack of children following us suddenly showed fear and retreated, in a rush.

This modest and moderately frank young man did not discuss the policy that had turned these people into camp inmates. That was a thing of the past; he was focused on the present. In his absorption in the task he had not stopped to reflect, evidently—nor had anyone else who was official—on what alternatives, really, the armed forces had had as to what to do with this mass of non-combatants once the decision had been made to clear the so-called Iron Triangle. Could they have been dumped into a field like human garbage and left to starve? *Something* had to be done with them, and quick, in view of public opinion. What *had* been done was not in any way meritorious, except in comparison to an atrocity. Yet seen through official eyes, misted over with sentiment, a cruel action was redeemed (school desks! six TV sets!) because its sequel was not as barbarous as someone might have reasonably expected. The briefing officers, telling the heart-moving "story" of Phu Cuong, showed a chuckling tenderness for the battle-weary American soldiers who had with their own hands helped those unfortunates move their pitiful furniture and animals—a great TV episode, replete with homely, humorous touches, squealing pigs, cackling hens, and a baby being born, surely, with a sergeant acting as midwife.

The hero of the Phu Cuong story is American know-how, American generosity, Uncle Sam with candy in his pockets. And Uncle Sam, like so many benefactors, is misunderstood. At lunch in his house, the local JUSPAO official expressed hurt and bewilderment over a New York *Times* story about Phu Cuong. The reporter had interviewed several refugees and printed what they told him; he quoted one woman as saying that she wished she were dead. "But that's natural," I objected. "Her husband had been killed by the Americans, and she'd lost her home and everything she had." "He ought to have given a cross-section," the man said in injured tones. "It creates the wrong picture of the camp." "If only one woman out of five wished she were dead, you're lucky," I said. But he was not persuaded. The story was unfair, he repeated. He actually wanted to think that the évacués in the camp were *happy*.

This lunatic attitude is widespread, though not always so doggedly stated. In their command posts, where the RVN flag proudly waves over what was recently a VC hamlet, American troops like to see smiling faces around them and hear the hum of reviving crafts and trades. The army band plays during Med Call in a half-reconstructed dispensary, to get the population to march up and take its medicine cheerfully; if no one comes, the Psy-war man is disconcerted. It is taken as a good sign (fortune is smiling) if the market reopens in a hamlet to which the population is inching back, though how the few inhabitants who return could be expected to live at all without a market for the exchange of vegetables, fish, rice, ducks is not clear. But to the men in occupation, the market proves that the hamlet *likes* the Army or the Marines. Not only do the Americans like to be liked

—the major clumping through the marketplace while the kids crowd around him shouting "You Number One," meaning "You're tops"—they want the local people to feel that the Americans like *them.* The Marine Corps recently gave a questionnaire to Marines and to Vietnamese. The results showed that only 46 per cent of the Vietnamese felt that "Americans like them as people," while a much larger percentage—65 or 70—said they liked Marines. A very sad situation, which the Marine Corps will have to get to work on, using its talent for public relations.

Of course there is a reason for this campaign to win friends. The strategists want the villagers to run and tell the nice captain when a VC attack is planned and to inform on their neighbors who are suspected Viet Cong sympathizers. You will be told by some vibrant officer that the people in his area have begun to "co-operate" with the Americans—the word "collaborate" is avoided—and yet his purpose in telling you this, jubilant and hand-rubbing, is confused. Is he glad that some old man has denounced his neighbor (quite possibly a private enemy) because this shows that security is increasing or because it is a sign that his command is well liked personally? Sometimes the second seems to dominate, especially when the officer is the "sincere" type who sees himself as bringing security to the hamlets he patrols, when practically he ought to be seeing himself as guaranteeing security to his troops. Such complex self-deception goes back perhaps to the old Indian fighting, where an Indian who liked white men was a good Indian: "an outstanding individual."

To some of the men fighting in Vietnam, naturally, there are no good Vietnamese except dead ones. They do not care about smiling faces; they want results—hard information delivered on the line. These are the Marines and other forces who stand by, watching noncommittally, while an ARVN soldier beats a captive girl: such a scene—one was described to me by a veteran artist commissioned to do war sketches who had witnessed it that afternoon—permits the man in uniform, puffing on a cigarette or chewing his cud of gum, to despise *all* Vietnamese equally. But in my experience the average soldier in Vietnam, when not fighting, is rather kindly—at least in those companies working on "pacification." He looks up and grins ("Morning, Ma'am") as he shows two slant-eyed kids how to fill sandbags to protect an artillery installation. It may not occur to him that his little helpers' fathers may be with the VC, 350 meters away, across the bridge from which sounds of a fire-fight are coming; if it does, what the hell? The kids are having fun.

If you tell an American official that the camp at Phu Cuong is a showcase, he is indignant. Of course it is a showcase, but the Americans don't like the word because it seems to impugn their motives. They will not even allow that their motives might be mixed. If you called it a pilot project, they would not mind. They also object if you call Phu Cuong a concentration camp, though that is what it is: these people have been arbitrarily rounded up and detained there, behind barbed wire, subjected to interrogation, and informers have been placed among them. To our officials, the term "concentration camp" has been copyrighted by the Nazis and automatically produces an image of jailers making lampshades of human skin—which they *know* is not happening at Phu Cuong. The barbed wire is there, they explain patiently, to protect the camp from the Viet Cong, but if the "refugees" are Viet Cong dependents, it is hard to imagine why their husbands and fathers would attack them with mortars and hand grenades.

In no respect is Phu Cuong a typical refugee camp, whether our authorities whose job is to deal with refugees are aware of the fact or not. To maintain that it is would be like saying that Mr. Lodge's (now Mr. Bunker's) residence is a typical Vietnamese dwelling. The fresh-water supply puts it in a class by itself, in my experience; so do the latrines, the school, the electricity, the TV sets, the garbage pickup points, the brand-new tin roofing, the relatively substantial daily food ration, the possibility of earning money by working, the quantity of household furniture, as well as the new American pajama sets the children are wearing and that were probably donated by some voluntary agency. Perhaps there are other refugee camps that have one or two of these features, but I have not heard of them. I can only speak of what I saw, in the north, near Hoi An, where I was taken by a group of German volunteers—the Catholic Knights of Malta—who were eager to have me see what *they* considered, after several months in the field, typical refugee camps. They did not show me what they called "the worst ones," because they were too hard to get to, which suggests that almost nobody sees them but visiting medical teams.

I had met these young Germans at Hue, in the University compound, where they were spending the evening with the German Professor of Medicine, who had organized the Medical School, and his wife—a real German evening, with Vietnamese *schnapps*, fresh sugared ginger, Schumann on the tape recorder, reminiscences of Jaspers (the doctor had been his student at Heidelberg), consultation of art books, to look up examples of Bavarian rococo and Rhineland "double" churches. The next morning, which was Sunday, the young people showed me the leper house in Hue, which they had been trying to clean up and humanize—a one-story structure, surrounded by mud, that may once have been a cow stable or a pigsty and that now housed seventy persons, lepers and their families. The Germans had installed electric lights, paved a dirt passageway directly in front of the hovel, washed the inside walls. You could not do much more, they said, as long as the lepers were living there. A tall, reddish-haired, round-featured electrical engineer from Cologne named Wolfgang surveyed the rusty screens full of holes, the stained walls, the dark dormitory where the women were crowded (one of the electrical fixtures was not working, he noted), the dirty floor; he sighed. Then he took me outside to show me the overflowing cesspool that had been located just outside the small room where the lepers ate. A sickening smell of human excrement came from the regurgitating cesspool and from the latrine a few feet away. Next to the cesspool, outside the kitchen, where some food was being warmed, was a heap of uncollected garbage. A few chickens were stalking around the garbage heap, and some ducks were swimming in muddy water that had collected in a depression in the yard. Wolfgang and his friends were discouraged. The head of the Hue hospital disapproved of their efforts. "Why are you giving things to those lepers?" he had told them. "They are all VC."

The young Knights of Malta, boys and girls, had conceived the project of moving the lepers into a decent building. They had secured an old hospital pavilion the town government had condemned; they had carpentered, wired, painted (the outside was now a pale cream-yellow), installed ventilating equipment, which they had had to buy because the head of the hospital had tried to sell them the old equipment for a much higher price, it turned out, than they had had to pay for new ventilators on the market. Then, as soon as they had installed it, the whole ventilating system was stolen, over a weekend—by the hospital electrician, the police reckoned. So it was all to do over, and meanwhile the lepers were still in the filthy old leper house, with their families, including some children who were not lepers, on the Vietnamese live-in system, and including also, Wolfgang confided, one or two that he thought were pseudo-lepers, who lived in the leprosarium and rented their houses—a pitiful case of graft.

They received from the government a daily ration of rice, a little meat, and occasionally bananas. "Not enough," said Wolfgang, shaking his head. In a small workshop, some of them wove on frames the pale, wide, conical hats that are a specialty of Hue, to sell on the market. When we visited, it was Têt, so that no one was working; the men, some lacking a finger, were playing cards, and the women were lying or crouching on their wooden beds, without bedclothes—one was dying. They showed us the little Buddhist and Catholic altars they had decorated for the New Year.

As a supplement, the Knights of Malta gave me a quick tour of the Hue madhouse, known as the "psychiatric wing" of the hospital. Here conditions were more terrible than in the leprosarium. A few sane children of insane mothers were roaming about the dirty, untended female ward; a depressive sat howling on her bed. Rusty torn screens, fly-splattered walls. There was no sign of a nurse; no patient had been washed or combed. At the entrance to the dangerous ward, old tin cans were lying in the mud. A madman stared out of a peephole; the place was locked, and no one could go in because, at least today, there were no attendants. It was worse before, the Knights of Malta said, when the government used to put political opponents here.

Seeing the Hue leper house and this bedlam somewhat readied me for the "temporary" refugee camps I was shown the next day, in Cam Chau, outside Hoi An. The first of these camps was about six months old and contained 1,500 people. As I walked with a German doctor through rows of communal huts, we came to a stagnant duck pond, about ten or fifteen feet wide, in which some ducklings in fact were swimming amid floating tin cans and other refuse. This was the water facility—the *only* water for drinking, washing, and cooking, to supply 700 people. On the other side of the camp, which was divided in two, was another duck pond, perhaps slightly larger, which served the remaining 800. There were no sanitary facilities of any kind; we saw women and children squatting; garbage was strewn in front of the huts, which had earth floors and inflammable old straw roofing. Yet *The Reporter* dated January 12 was telling its readers in a reassuring article that seems to have sprung, full-blown, from a briefing session that Dr. Que, "a doctor by training" and head of the Vietnamese refugee bureau, has "established standards for sanitation and medical attention in refugee camps." It is true that the writer does not say what the standards are.

The misery and squalor of that first camp is hard to convey, partly because the eye shrinks from looking too closely at it, as though out of respect for the privacy of those who are enduring such disgrace. The women stood massed in their doorways to watch us pass; some approached the doctor and asked for medicine. But mostly they just watched us, defying us, I felt, to watch *them.* Skin diseases were rampant, especially among the children, diseases of the scalp, eye diseases, gross signs of malnutrition, bad teeth, stained by betel-chewing and reduced, often, to stumps. Most of the refugees (as usual women and children and a few grandfathers) were dirty—how could they wash? In contrast to the new American-made seersuckers and ginghams of Phu Cuong, the pajamas of the children here were old, torn, discolored. The daily food allowance of ten piasters per family, supplemented irregularly by a little rice, said the doctor, was below subsistence requirements. Some families had begun straggly little vegetable patches—mainly lettuce plants, cabbage, and mustard—that were growing haphazardly amidst the refuse. This would help a little. And there were a few pigs, chickens, and the ducklings. But except for this spasmodic gardening, there was no work for these people—no fields they could plant, nothing. The Knights of Malta had procured a mechanical saw, in the hope of giving work to the able-bodied older men and teaching a trade to the boys, but owing to Vietnamese bureaucratic stubbornness, the young carpenter, who had left his job in Germany to come here, like the others, for a year, had not been authorized to take apprentices. This tall pale embodiment of German conscientiousness was working alone in his "shop" in province headquarters, sawing perfect boards, like some woodcut figure in a folk tale from the Black Forest, while outside the window an idle company of Popular Forces, in black pajamas, watched him all day long and giggled. The Knights of Malta were disgusted. "Maybe I will just *draft* some of the refugees," said the baron from the Rhineland, a graduate in agriculture, who was the head of the team.

These Germans were full of outspoken Christian indignation at what they were witnessing at close quarters. "Nobody could be more opposite than Germans and Vietnamese," said a Canadian Jesuit tolerantly; he had watched the German medical faculty in Hue trying to make some headway against dirt and local corruption. The Viet Cong, he said, would clean up that hospital in a day by simply shooting the chief grafters—a course that seemed to appeal to him as a man but not as a priest; as a priest, he counseled patience.

But the Knights of Malta were right to be scandalized. They had volunteered, it turned out, for a labor of Hercules and Sisyphus rolled into one. Yet at the same time, of all the Westerners I saw in Vietnam, only these German boys and girls (in particular, Wolfgang, the electrician) showed gentleness and compassion with the small, fragile Vietnamese, stroking a leper's shoulder, respectfully helping an old man scramble up to show the writing on a Buddhist altar. "You gimme cigarette!" a very small Vietnamese boy said to a young Knight, who refused and added in apology: "It is not good that they smoke."

The next camp they showed me was divided into three sections: Catholic, Buddhist, and Cao Dai—in all, about 4,500 people. It had been in existence over a year and was "better." That is, the huts had tin roofs and cement floors; the vegetable-growing was much more extensive, and the rows of seedlings—lettuces, cabbages, mustard greens, beans, onion sets, tomato plants —better cared for and neater. Some camp leadership had developed. But again there was the water question. A well had finally been dug. As we passed, the doctor bent down and sniffed it. He made a face. "It's tainted?" He nodded. "Do they boil the water for cooking?" "We have told them. Then we watch to see if they will boil it. . . ." He raised his shoulders in a shrug.

This camp had a few more pigs, piglets, and chickens, a few more ducklings; in the field behind, some water buffalo belonging to the refugees were grazing. But here again the garbage was all-pervasive. There were no latrines, and again we saw skin diseases, eye diseases, every kind of scurfy and scabious sore, swollen stomachs, protruding bones, rickets. There was no school and no work for the refugees, except in the tiny garden plots between the serried huts. Some were growing flowers—marigolds. The doctor, a man in his fifties, seemed to think that the Catholic section was in better order than the Buddhist section, but I could not see any difference. All the children in this camp were more disciplined than in the newer camp, where the doctor had had to speak to them bluntly to keep them from hitting and pushing me, not altogether in play—at any rate they had not thrown stones at me, as they did in one "pacified" hamlet, when the briefing officer was not looking.

We did not see the Cao Dai section because someone came to tell the doctor that a plague case had been reported in a nearby hamlet. He left. One of the German women stood sentinel while I went to the toilet (which did not lock or have a light) in the province headquarters; it was going to be a long drive in the Red Cross station wagon back to the base at Da Nang. On the way home, I remarked to the baron that, though conditions were appalling even in the "better" camp, I did not see that they were much worse than in the hamlets we were passing through and in others I had visited in Vietnam. Except for water. Water and work, he said. Otherwise there was not too much difference. The diseases in the camps were the same as the diseases in the hamlets; it was only that the crowding in the camps made epidemics more likely. And, having no work, the people had less to eat. Another bad feature of the situation was that the people in the hamlets looked down on the refugees—there were 150,000 in the province—and would not have anything to do with them.

In the hamlets, I had noticed, houses were sometimes quite clean on the inside, but outside there was the same filthy jetsam that you saw in the camps. I wondered if it had always been like this in Vietnam. The baron did not know. It seemed unlikely to me that the Vietnamese, who have the reputation of being an industrious people, could have lived in such conditions for centuries. One got the impression that a lapse into degradation had occurred in fairly recent times, just as there had been a lapse into illiteracy: before the French came, according to Donald Lancaster, the English Indo-Chinese historian, the rural population had been literate; the French had wiped that out systematically in the nineteenth century.

At any rate, one thing was clear. Before the Americans came, there could have been no rusty Coca-Cola or beer cans or empty whiskey bottles. They had brought them. It was this indestructible mass-production garbage floating in swamps and creeks, lying about in fields and along the roadside that made the country, which must once have been beautiful, hideous. In the past, the "natural" garbage created by human beings and animals must have been reabsorbed by the landscape, like compost—fish bones, chicken bones, rice husks, dry bamboo, eggshells, vegetable peelings, excreta. The American way of life has donated this disfiguring industrial garbage to the Asian countryside, which is incapable of digesting it. And anyone who wishes to make a comparison, in Asian terms, has only to get a tourist visa for Cambodia, where the people are far less industrious and where even in the poorest sections of the capital and in remote hamlets everything is clean.

Only in Hue, the old imperial capital of Annam, can you see what Vietnam must have looked like—dignified and melancholy—before the Americans came. There is scarcely any motor traffic; the Perfumed River is lined with dark sampans; the women, in traditional costume, carry the traditional twin baskets balanced on a pole. The reason is simple: Hue is off limits to U.S. troops, a pariah city. This is intended to be a punishment for the fighting and demonstrations during the Buddhist Struggle Movement in May-June 1966, when the USIS library was burned down by angry students. As a punishment, too, the corpse of the library has been allowed to stand near the center of the city, a You-Did-It-Yourself memorial. The few official Americans left in Hue—some OCO men, a JUSPAO man, a CIA man—with a small Vietnamese policeman on guard before each of their houses (there was no policeman to keep an eye on the lepers' pavilion), point out the blackened ruin with steely satisfaction: Hue is paying for its sins by being cut off from U.S. culture. You would think from their grim tone it was Auschwitz or Buchenwald, standing as a permanent lesson. Despite suggestions from the

University that it would be wiser to rebuild the library, the Americans, so far, have declined. Yet some U.S. culture, in the wider sense, can still be found in Hue. On a Sunday morning, I saw three middle-aged gun-toting civilians resembling Yukon prospectors alight from their car outside the sanctuary of the Emperors' Tombs, where Vietnamese were slowly walking under parasols around the lotus trees and pools filled with green plants and covered with a pale green scum. The three construction workers (I had seen them the day before in the hotel at Hue and was told they were engineers, probably, from the base at Phu Bai) advanced through the gates with a PX shopping bag full of beer cans. They were raising the first cans to their lips as they strode on toward the tombs and pagodas, which were guarded by gods and stone elephants. Where they tossed the empties, I cannot say.

Near any large American base in Vietnam, the countryside resembles nothing more than a dump or the lepers' pigyard, with backed-up cesspool, I would say, except that the lepers are too poor to afford Miller's High Life and too suspect politically to receive canned surplus products. Even the B-52's will not be able to "sterilize the area," since cans are not combustible. They can be flattened out, and a form of Pop Art is spreading in rural Vietnam; new house fronts (not just in refugee camps) are made of flattened-out cans, sometimes in bright patterns, as with beer, ginger ale, and Coca-Cola containers, and sometimes in plain old tin, as with corned beef hash and Campbell's soup. Yet even if every hut and hovel in Vietnam were faced with this new building material, it would hardly reduce the vast rubbish heap, the fecal matter of our civilization, we have left in the country. As our troops increase, there will be more and more.

Not to mention another kind of garbage. As we approached Da Nang, the baron pointed to some wreckage a few yards from the road. An American bomber had crashed there a few months ago, he said, killing eighty-one people. The crash was due to mechanical failure, which perhaps means that the eighty-one people should not be counted as war casualties but as simple victims of an accident, like the children burned by gasoline stoves (because of the kerosene shortage) or by the straw roofs and cardboard sidings catching fire in a crowded refugee camp, who must be carefully distinguished from children burned by napalm. The bomber wreck was lying with one wing atilt, its nose buried in a roof, amid the splinters of houses or buildings. Nobody had bothered to inter it. There was another one a few miles off, the baron said. He was not sure how many people it had killed.

Back in the Marine Press Base, there were Martinis-on-the-rocks, steaks, *vin rosé*, cognac. Behind the restaurant counter was a sign: "Have you taken your weekly malaria pill? Help yourself." And the Marines were all very nice, really nice, both officers and men; they asked what I had seen and was it interesting. Conditions were unspeakable, I said, mentioning the first camp's water supply. They nodded, hitched up chairs, as though they were glad to get the lowdown on those camps. And being Americans, they were disturbed to hear about the dirty water. As well as pleased to learn that the German team had paid them a compliment: the Marines, the baron told me, had been very helpful about getting them supplies and transport sometimes for the wounded.

The Marines' receptiveness was strikingly different from the behavior of civilian bureaucrats in Saigon, who, I discovered, did not want to hear about conditions in refugee camps; they stopped listening after the first words and picked up the telephone ("Excuse me a minute") or assumed an abstracted air, as though they were thinking of something more important—the Viet Cong weekly atrocity statistics perhaps. What was curious about the Marines' attitude was that they were interested, but in the way civilians back home might be interested—"You don't say!" Or as though they were leafing through a copy of the *National Geographic* and had hit on an item about a place they had been to on a world tour or a business trip. The same mild interest in "keeping up" that made them subscribe to news magazines and frown over photographs of the floods in Florence.

Whereas the civilian officials, on the whole, behaved like a team of promoters with a dubious "growth" stock they were brokering, many of the military, like these Marines, remained singularly detached, seeming to feel no need to justify the American presence or their own involvement, unconcerned with selling the war (for they in fact were not the salesmen but the product). The Marine colonel at his command post could say forthrightly, "We created the refugees"—something no civilian official would dare to admit, and quite rightly. They could tell stories out of school about Vietnamese corruption and thievery, which they regarded as almost universal, criticize the Chieu Hoi program, mock the ARVN, all this without noticing that if what they were saying was true the public rationale for American intervention disappeared. The Information officers behind them were more sensitive to the dangers of such free talk on the part of their superiors and tried, if possible, to forestall it. In a hamlet in the delta one morning, I asked some army officers what the local government had done about land reform; the briefing captain hurriedly opened his mouth and started to recite some figures, when the colonel cut in—"*Nothing.*"

It may be that the Information officers, whose job is to give the reverse of information ("How many of the inhabitants have come back to Rach Kien?" Briefing captain: "About a thousand." Field major, half an hour later: "632"), are more honest, in a way, than the field officers who burst out with the truth. That is, the blunt colonels and sympathetic majors have not been able to realize that this is a war, unlike World War II or the Korean War, in which the truth must not be told, except when it cannot be hidden. Even then it must be turned upside down or restyled, *viz.*, "the problems of success," which also comprised inflation. Those who lie and cover up are implicitly acknowledging this, in some recess of their souls, while the outspoken field officer still lets himself think he is fighting the kind of war where an honest officer can gripe.

In reality, he gives away *less* than the double-talking U.S. bureaucrat in Saigon, who has the answers ready before you can ask the question, who can give you, straight as a die, the chemical formula for the defoliants, harmless to pets and humans, we have begun that day, he announces, to use in the DMZ (as though he had no inkling of the fact previously announced by him—has it slipped his mind?—that we have been bombing the Zone regularly for some time), who when asked if he can supply you with some figures on civilian casualties says no, unfortunately not; there are none, but offers you instead statistics on Viet Cong terror, who, like Johnson's emissary (now civilian head of "pacification"), can declare "simply" to the press, to back up an optimistic estimate: "I feel a new sensa confidence in the air." A discovery I have made in Vietnam is that those who seek to project an "image" are unaware of how they look. The truth they are revealing has become invisible to them.

One example of this revealing blindness can illustrate. In the OCO offices in Saigon, I was offered a freshly typed list of Viet Cong acts of terror committed during the previous week; as the reader must have gathered, this material seems to be the favorite reading of our spokesmen. That and infiltration figures, to give the "background." As I looked down the list I noticed that it included an attack on a U.S. army post! "Is that terrorism?" I wondered, pointing. The official studied the item. "No. It doesn't belong there," he admitted, poring over the type-sheet with a mystified air, like one awakening from a dream. "We'll have to correct that," he added briskly. It was clear that he had offered me those figures in *good faith,* having seen nothing wrong with them; to him an attack on a U.S. army unit, even in wartime, was dastardly.

At present the terror statistics issued to the newspapers are blandly including kidnappings and "murders" of Rural Construction workers, which sounds very atrocious if you do not know (as everyone in Saigon does) that Rural Construction is the old name for Revolutionary Development—the "workers" are paramilitary elements trained and drilled in a special school and sent to "cleanse" (U.S. word) "pacified" hamlets; of each team of fifty-nine, thirty-four are armed for security purposes, *i.e.*, to repel a Viet Cong attack. The sudden switch to the old name is like an alert to the press to watch out for the oncoming lie. Why, you ask, are they cooking these particular statistics?

What is behind it? What are they up to now? Such transparent subterfuges awaken not just disgust but pity for a fast-talking nation that seems to think it is addressing itself to punchcards and mimeograph machines; even a computer, which has memory —if not reason—would jib.

Intellectuals

"Il faut une *REVOLUTION!*" Major Be said, letting the *r* roll like a cannon ball in the school at Vung Tau. The Italian general listened with an air of dawning surprise. The short broad-faced Vietnamese major was not a military chieftain of the NLF, but the head of the government school for Revolutionary Development, training anti-Communist cadres. The former Italian Chief of Staff and I were being briefed in French by Major Be in a small classroom, while in the next room a group from NBC was being briefed in English by his assistant, Mr. Chau. Thin, slight Mr. Chau, dressed in flowing black calico trousers and a tight black tunic resembling an alb, had taken a degree in English literature at the Sorbonne—he had done his doctoral thesis on Virginia Woolf. Major Be, less at home in foreign languages, wore a black shirt open at the throat and black trousers cut like army fatigues. Their costumes were symbolic of the aims of the program. The 3,000 cadres now in the school (a cadre is one person), when they graduated, would start "constructing" hamlets in teams of fifty-nine, wearing the black-pajama garb of the Viet Cong, which itself had been copied from the dress of the poor peasants. Actually, the peasants today in government-controlled areas wear a medley of clothes, including baseball caps, shorts, and T-shirts; and the RD getup, I heard from a Vietnamese medical student, was regarded as ludicrous in the hamlets he had been visiting during Têt—"If they would only take off those silly pajamas, the people might not laugh at them."

"*Vraiment une révolution,*" Major Be insisted. The Italian general cast an inquiring look at me. "*Qu'est-ce qu'il veut dire par ça?*" he murmured. I did not know what Major Be had in mind when he said that his country had to have a revolution, though I agreed with him, whatever he meant. It was monotonous to hear everywhere the same stories of graft and thieving at the expense of the poor; only yesterday an unusually frank OCO man had been telling about what had happened with a distribution of clothing donated through AID—the best clothes had been pilfered by the authorities and never reached the needy. To receive aid at all, he said sadly, poor families had to qualify as needy with the government. "You mean they had to pay to qualify as needy?" He looked at me in silence, by way of an answer.

Still, the briefing I had already had in Saigon on the RD program had hardly prepared me to meet a doctrinaire theoretician of the type of Major Be, who, warming to his subject, was now assuring us that Vietnamese society was "*complètement corrompue*": the ruling classes, he said, as the general's eyes widened, had always used the laws to serve their own interests. Then, glancing at his watch, he switched to facts and figures.

The program had been started in December 1965. Twenty-eight thousand cadres were already in the field. The school training period lasted twelve weeks, during which each cadre accomplished eleven tasks and went through twelve stages. Upon graduation, each cadre team would work with a hamlet to establish or maintain eleven criteria; an additional nine criteria, achieved with cadre support, would turn a constructed or Old Life Hamlet into a New Life Hamlet. Good results had not yet been produced, but the program was on the way—"*dans la bonne direction.*"

General Liuzzi was too new in the country to be up on some of the terminology. A "constructed" hamlet meant not a newly built one but a former Viet Cong hamlet that had been worked over politically to the point where it could now be considered pro-government. A "reconstructed" hamlet meant one that had been "constructed" and then backslid and had had to be "constructed" all over again, but this term, for some reason, had fallen into disfavor, and a "reconstructed" hamlet was now called a "consolidated" hamlet. Finally the goal of each was to become a "real New Life Hamlet."

A "constructed" hamlet backslid because a poor job had been done in rooting out the Viet Cong "infrastructure." Rooting out the "infrastructure," *i.e.*, conducting purges, was the most important task of Major Be's cadres. Major Be, to give him credit, did not use the expression, though the American briefers in Saigon had used it, repeatedly. That word, too freshly minted to be in my dictionary, is already a worn slug in American Vietnamese, tirelessly inserted into dinner-table conversations, briefings, newspaper and magazine articles. Its primary meaning is that the person using it (succinctly or sententiously, depending) has an up-to-date scientific grasp of the workings of underground Communism—a meaning that could not be conveyed by the word "organization" or even "cells." It is not restricted to the few—Harvard political science graduates or Princetonian school-of-government captains; it is as democratic as a subway token. One would not be surprised to hear it mumbled by some high-school dropout as he cleaned his weapon: "Got to get Charlie's infrastructure." To our propaganda men, who like to write of "the faceless Viet Cong" (sometimes appending their photographs), "infrastructure," aside from sounding knowledgeable and hard-headed, probably suggests infra-red—invisible rays just beyond red in the political spectrum.

Major Be and Mr. Chau are the Vietnamese counterparts of the American political scientists who have stamped their vocabulary and their habits of thought on this loony trial of strength in the Asian arena. Here for the first time, political science, as taught and studied in the big American universities, is being applied to war, where it often seems close to science fiction. Such a thing was scarcely dreamed of in World War II, despite the presence of a few professors and intellectuals in the OWI and OSS—no one thought of "studying" the Nazis and learning from them. Only the physical scientists became an auxiliary of the Defense Department. The present phenomenon, more portentous for the future, if there is one, than Dr. Strangelove—conceivably you can outlaw the Bomb, but what about the Brain?—dates back to the Cold War, when the "science" of Kremlinology was discovered. The sinister Walt Rostow, said now to be closest to the cupped presidential ear, dates back also to that Age of Discovery. The behavior of the enemy was studied under university microscopes, with the aid of samples furnished by defectors to the Free World. Practical experiment, however, was not really feasible until the war in Vietnam provided a laboratory for testing the new weapon, an academic B-52 or Lazy Dog. Watching it operate in Vietnam, in conjunction with the sister "disciplines" of sociology and anthropology ("The Vietnamese don't know how to handle them," an American evangelical missionary kindly "filled in" a reporter, alluding to the Montagnard tribes the VC was winning over. "They have no anthropology to guide them"), you wonder whether this branch of knowledge can ever have been designed for anything but war. The notion of a "pure" political science here seems as remote from actuality as atoms-for-peace.

Right after the Geneva Accords, the paramilitary professors began moving into Vietnam, the first being Diem's inventor, Professor Wesley Fishel, of Michigan State. But as long as Eisenhower was in office, the academic expertise on Vietnam remained rather old-fogyish, like the prudent Eisenhower himself. Though the United States gave a large subsidy to Michigan State University to train a Vietnamese police force and to form Vietnamese adepts in Political Science and Public Administration, this, after all, was classic colonial practice. A new wrinkle —Civics 303?—was the addition of some undercover CIA men to the Michigan State faculty (they had academic rank but not tenure apparently), to start a Vietnamese Bureau of Investigation on the model of the FBI. But on the whole the MSU alumni and alumnae you still find in Vietnamese government nooks—nearly every Vietnamese who speaks English seems to have attended Michigan State and to be proud of it—have a certain démodé pathos, like the bangled, coquettish Dr. Hue, Professor of Public Administration at the National Institute of Administration in Saigon, who resembles a road-show revival of Madame Nhu. Professor Fishel's lasting contribution was not Nhu's CIA-trained Secret Police—where are they now?—but the introduction of the word "semantics" into official discourse about Vietnam. "We do ourselves and our Asian neighbors harm when we insist on stretching or shrinking them into our particular semantic bed," he wrote in *The New Leader,* arguing for a "new political vocabulary" in an article wonderfully entitled (Professor Fishel claims by the editors) "Vietnam's Democratic One-Man Rule"—the Procrustean subject was Diem. A democratic "dictator" or a "democratic" dictator? Words failed Professor Fishel. Diem has gone, but embarrassments of the kind he created have not. Almost daily in the press briefing, whenever a newsman raises his hand to ask for clarification of some mealymouthed statement: "I am not going to debate semantics with you," the spokesman replies. "Next?"

It took the New Frontier, though, to really update American "thinking" on Vietnam. A fresh look at the situation by the Kennedy men revealed the need for brand-new tactics with brand-new names: counter-insurgency, special warfare. The notion of counter-insurgency in reality was borrowed from elite French officers who used it in Algeria—with what results, we know. To implement the new approach, and with CIA support, the Army created its Special Forces—the Green Berets—whose task was to combine unconventional fighting (counter-guerrilla activity) with political savvy. The Vietnamese, separate but equal, got *their* Special Forces—the Red Berets—a counter-terror group wearing leopard-spotted uniforms with a tiger's head on the breast pocket; they are still in action, bringing the severed heads of guerrillas or putative guerrillas into a pacified hamlet to show the shocked American colonel. Concurrently, a new, less narrow-minded type of officer appeared in the field, with a traveling library; on the bookshelves in his mountain hideout were the works of Mao, Generals Giap and Grivas, Ho

Chi Minh—doubtless in paperback. Young West Pointers were turned into political strategists on the spot by crash courses in Communism and native psychology, and *Webster's Collegiate Dictionary* was placed on the desk of an old-style general, for convenient reference. The same year—1961—that the Special Forces were created, the Staley Plan was devised by a Stanford economist, Eugene Staley, whose name is now identified with Strategic Hamlets, though his Plan, in fact, was much more comprehensive and undertook a complete restyling of the Vietnamese economy, the political struggle, and the AID program.

No ordinary desk official in Washington could have imagined the Staley Plan. The idea of Strategic Hamlets was not new in itself; Diem and his brother Nhu had founded agrovilles—basically, fortified settlements, also on an Algerian model—which at one time bore the name of Camps of the Just Cause. But Staley *perfected* the agrovilles.* With a professor's fondness for the diagram, he divided the country into yellow zones, blue zones, red zones, the yellow zones being governmental (available for U.S. aid), the blue dubious, and the red VC. His plan was to transfer the population, wherever movable, into Prosperity Zones, which were to contain 15,000 model hamlets, for a starter, all heavily fortified and surrounded by barbed wire. With the enthusiastic co-operation of General Maxwell Taylor (who is still testifying before the Senate as an authority on Vietnam), about 2,500 Staleyized hamlets were actually built. Life in them was diagrammed down to the last detail. Everyone was obliged to purchase and wear a uniform—four different color

* I owe this description of Strategic Hamlets to Kuno Knoebel's interesting book, *Victor Charlie*. A very different account is given by Roger Hillsman in *To Move a Nation*.

combinations, according to age and sex—and to carry two identity cards, one for moving about in the hamlet and the other for leaving it. The gates were closed by a guard every night at seven o'clock and opened at six in the morning. Persons consenting to be resettled in a strategic hamlet had their houses burned and crops sprayed with poison chemicals, so as to leave a razed area behind for the Viet Cong—this was the first widespread application of the science of chemistry to the political struggle. The U.S. government paid compensation, of course.

Those who did not agree to relocation were removed forcibly and their villages burned and sprayed anyway; some reluctant peasants and village elders were executed, as examples, by the Vietnamese army. Inside the hamlets, strict political control was exercised; executions took place here, too. The settlers were gouged for special taxes and other arbitrary impositions; the compensation money was not turned over to them in many instances. They were ordered to get any relations they had in the red zones to join them in the hamlet within three months; if they failed to recruit them, they were punished. Professor Staley, no doubt, was not responsible for the excesses of the program as implemented; he had *only* drawn a totalitarian blueprint for the Vietnamese and American advisers to follow, based on *his experience of the country*.

The Staley Plan proved to be the greatest gift the U.S. gave the Viet Cong. Naturally, revolts broke out in the strategic hamlets; sometimes the settlers put fire to them. When Diem fell, the program was dropped, and Professor Staley apparently went to Limbo, to join Professor Fishel. No one mentions them any more. But in fact the Strategic Hamlet idea reappeared, in less draconic form, in the Rural Construction program, which failed and was replaced by the Revolutionary Development program. Revolutionary Development adds the black pajamas, as a stiffener, to Rural Construction. And the black-pajama uniform proclaims a thing that was always implicit in such conceptions as counter-insurgency and special warfare and in some features of the Staley Plan—plagiarism of the enemy's techniques.

Indeed the "other" war dramatically declared by Johnson at Honolulu is an idea rather tardily lifted from the Viet Cong. Long before the Americans thought of it, the VC was building schools for the peasantry, digging wells, teaching better methods of agriculture. But because the Viet Cong did not control the mass media, the "secret" of its appeal remained a secret, at least from the military, who are digging the wells, building the schools, under the impression that this grass-roots courtship originated in the big heart of America. It would not occur to a general (unless he were Caesar) that he was plagiarizing from the enemy; to a straight-shooting man of action, the thought is distasteful.

And now here was Major Be, his slant eyes gleaming, talking about a "revolution," stealing the NLF's thunder to pass on to his cadres. Yet the NLF in its proclamations never speaks of revolution, but, instead, of "raising the living standards of the population," "economic progress without violent changes," a "campaign for freedom against repression," "forming a broad democratic base." That seems to have escaped Major Be's sponsors, who are sure they know what the NLF *really* intends—a complete Communist take-over. Let us say they are right. What follows is sheer comedy: the NLF aims at a social revolution, while taking care not to pronounce the word, and the South Vietnamese junta launches a program styled "revolutionary," while failing to institute the mildest reforms. The attempt on the part of the Americans and their local star pupils to turn this into a war of ideas is something to make the angels, if there are any, dry their tears and laugh.

In the next room, NBC had finished its briefing session. But Major Be, carried away by the courteous old general's slightly puzzled interest, was quoting Mao: "The water protects the fish." The people, he elucidated, were the water in which the guerrilla swam like a fish while the alien enemy drowned. Revolutionary Development was adapting Mao's proverb to fight the VC. The school at Vung Tau was a hatchery to breed little fish—the cadres—to protect the water, which in turn would protect the big fish, that is, the government forces.

I decided to ask about land reform. Land reform, said the major, was useless without a "cultural base" to support it. Western ideas were necessary and Western technology. On the other hand, the Vietnamese people must not be turned into beggars. A tractor in each hamlet would be the most beautiful symbol of modern civilization. The tractor; not the airplane and the bomber. The general nodded thoughtfully. He was impressed by Major Be. He inquired where he had studied, meaning, no doubt, where on earth he had learned his ideology. "*Mon université est la campagne vietnamienne,*" replied the stocky major, who was not forthcoming about his past. Mr. Chau, who was, had been until recently a professor of French and English literature at Hue University. Probably he had left in disgust during the Struggle Movement of the previous year. He was against

TV, Hondas, transistors, and other corrupting influences on Vietnamese youth.

We left the school buildings, which dated back to the French and had a monastic atmosphere, like a Jesuit seminary, with Major Be as the Father Superior, the organizing dynamo, and Mr. Chau, more scholastic, in his black habit, as the Prefect of studies. Major Be's predecessor as head of the Vung Tau school had been a different type—the guitar-playing Major Mai, whom the CIA was backing as a winner last year and who is now barely recollected by the American officials who once vigorously endorsed him. "What happened to Major Mai?" Gavin Young of *The Observer* asked a leading figure in the Embassy. "*Who?* Oh yes, him. Well, he didn't work out. Don't know where he is now." "That's strange. You were so enthusiastic about him last year." "Oh, I wouldn't say that, Gavin. You've got that wrong." "But I have it in my notes." "He was *on probation*, Gavin," the American said reproachfully. In the days of Major Mai, the theme at Vung Tau had been pure Vietnamese nationalism; the cadres got military training and close coaching in the story of the Dragon King and the Lady of the Fairies—the legendary parents of Vietnam—which was then the message designed to win the hearts and minds of the Vietnamese people. In those days the school had a corps of CIA advisers, dressed in black pajamas and sandals, except for their chief, who, as pictured by Young, was dressed and behaved like a deputy sheriff in Selma, Alabama, with cigar between his teeth, and sport shirt hanging out over his spilling belly. Now, however, there were no CIA men around, unless deeply disguised (though invisible American "advisers" were mentioned as among the cadres' teachers, and in fact the CIA is still backing the school), no Dragon King or Lady of the Fairies; there were only Major Be and "Virginia Woolf" and the teachings of Chairman Mao.

Out in the woods, we were taken to view the cadres. Here, said the major, indicating the sandy forest, theory was digested and turned into technique. Grouped on benches, in a large open hut, a class was receiving instruction from a native teacher and feeding it back in shouts, like a child's catechism: "Who made the world?" "God made the world." Or, as the brochures furnished to arriving journalists in their press kit present *our* sacred doctrine in easy question-and-answer form: "*Question:* Why is the United States waging war against North Vietnam? *Answer:* The U.S. is not doing that at all. We are helping the free government and people of the Republic of Vietnam defend their freedom and independence against aggression, directed and in part supplied from North Vietnam. . . . *Question:* How have the Viet Cong managed to gain and hold control over parts of South Vietnam? *Answer:* The Viet Cong rule by force and terror. Deliberate killings and kidnappings are instruments of their policy. . . . *Question:* Do the Viet Cong attack only South Vietnamese soldiers and civilian officials? *Answer:* By no means. The Viet Cong also attack teachers, agricultural technicians, anti-malaria teams—anybody, in fact, who is working to improve social and economic conditions in South Vietnam." Some Vietnamese version of this kind of thing was what the cadres in the forest were chanting. Major Be did not interpret. In Major Mai's time, the instruction went as follows: "*Question:* Are the Americans our friends if they defend the nation of the Great

King Hung Vuong, son of the Dragon? *Answer:* Yes. *Question:* Are they our masters? *Answer:* Never."

Next, the cadres were lined up in military formation and drilled. To each order, they responded with a terrifying howl. As he surveyed the trainees, the Italian general's enthusiasm cooled; very poor-grade military material, he observed. In Saigon, a Vietnamese girl had dismissed the whole outfit as "draft dodgers"—a common view—but though some of these unprepossessing youths were evidently of military age, many would have been dismissed as unfit for military service anywhere, and as for the sad, somnolent, gray-haired grandfathers in the ranks, whatever had caused them to enlist in this pathetic brigade of "revolutionary" youth, it cannot have been fear of the draft.

We asked Major Be what qualifications a cadre had to have to be admitted to the school. All had to be literate, he said, and each new cadre had to be sponsored by two full-fledged member cadres—a system patterned on that of the NLF and the People's Revolutionary Party and suited to a clandestine organization or secret fraternity. Evidently, an effort was being made to invest the cadres with the aura of an initiate, through ritual and the abracadabra of numbers. Each team, when it went into a hamlet (where it would spend three to six months), would be given ninety-eight "works" to accomplish; thirty-four cadres (this figure is sometimes given as thirty-three) would be detailed to security, nineteen to general staff, one to agriculture, one to co-operatives, one to construction and public works, one to public health, one to education and culture, one to grievance and public investigation. Given this division of labor, it was not surprising that I had never been able to see the RD cadres actually doing anything in a hamlet, except lounging around with a weapon or eating. Yet their training was evidently successful in instilling an elite spirit, to the extent that complaints of their "arrogance" and "insolence" are mentioned even in Vietnamese government reports.

As it is turning out, some of these "draft dodgers" would be safer in the ARVN: recent newspaper stories are full of the killings—always described as "murders"—of RD workers, who, despite their military training and the arms they carry, have been incapable of defending themselves in the hamlets they are assigned to against VC raids. Probably their overbearing ways make them popular targets.

The classes were breaking for lunch when a BBC cameraman arrived to film them. NBC was only taking notes. They reformed, to sing us a few stanzas of their school song; its theme was the eleven tasks, twelve stages. Most of the cadres in the forest were in Stage Two or Three. Twelve weeks, said the Italian general, regarding this performance, would not be enough. He eyed Major Be with misgiving. *"C'est un fanatique,"* he summed up, shaking his head. He would have liked to believe in Major Be. At lunch in the mess hall, talk turned to negotiations. Major Be's face darkened. *"La sale manoeuvre de la paix du pape,"* he said. The Pope's dirty peace trick. General Liuzzi refused the soup.

Across the table, Mr. Chau spoke contemptuously of South Vietnamese students in Paris who discussed and argued with North Vietnamese students. I defended them. *"La politique n'est pas un salon,"* he said in a venomous tone. To him, debate in politics, let alone compromise, was decadent, like formalism in art to an orthodox member of the Union of Soviet Writers. Here, as often in Vietnamese government circles, the mere word "*negotiations*" was enough to make a mask of cordiality drop.

Possibly "Virginia Woolf" and the major should be classed as fascists (as someone has put it, revolutionary slogans minus a revolution equals fascism), despite or even because of their likeness to doctrinaire Communists of the unreconstructed Stalinist type. Major Be's beautiful tractor advanced toward us out of the final sequence of an old Soviet movie, and "the Pope's dirty peace trick" could have been spat out equally well in Albania or possibly Peking. What had led this ascetic pair to work with the Americans was difficult to guess, especially in the case of the fastidious Mr. Chau, who clearly detested everything connected with the American way of life, everything soft, flabby, superfatted, PX-distributed.

The Italian general elicited that Major Be had fought with the Viet Minh against the French, which meant he had served under Giap; he seemed to be a Northerner who had come south at some unstated time. The pure and unyielding principles of Hanoi exercise an attraction on the displaced intellectuals who fled the scene, including those who are most fanatically anti-Communist. The day after I visited Vung Tau, I met another "revolutionary," manifestly sincere, an army captain and acting district chief who in former life had been a private French teacher and a portrait photographer, like Ho, whose province he came from. He was eager for me to explain to the Americans, who might not understand, that it was "*le peuple, le bas peuple*" that mattered, not the government bureaucracy (of which he was an element) or the people on top. In the U.S. army command post, a salient in VC territory, he seized a ballpoint and drew diagrams. One, a pyramid with a demagogue on top and an unstable base, was "no good" (he illustrated how it could fall over); the other, a squat trapezoid, with a broad base, the people, on which a flat top rested, was good. The American junior officers listened indulgently; they had evidently heard all this before and considered him a visionary, though "a great guy." His views and didactic excitement reminded me of Major Be, and I asked him what he thought of Revolutionary Development. To my surprise, he disapproved. "*En toute franchise,*" he said, the school at Vung Tau was a perfect illustration of the "bad" pyramid. He also disapproved of the Constitutional Assembly: too much talk, he said, and too many competing blocs. Like Major Be, he spurned any thought of negotiations. He dreamed only of victory: "The march on Hanoi!" The Americans grinned and shook their heads; they had heard this before, too, and were not buying it. He looked hurt.

His case was typical. Many South Vietnamese have a double fear of the Americans: that, despite what they say, the Americans are there to take over their country, and that the Americans will betray them by making peace with Hanoi. That is, they are torn between the fear that the Americans will stay and the fear that they will go. It was the same with the French. Irredentists like the ex-photographer look back with trembling horror on "*le jour d'infâme*"—July 20, 1954, the infamous day of the Geneva Accords. Perhaps those who are working directly with the CIA, like Major Be and Mr. Chau, feel less distrust of their saviors than those who are obliged to work with the regular Army, which, in their eyes, is less reliable politically. And from their point of view they may be right. The Army, like all armies, basically wants to go home, while the CIA wants to stay, discreetly behind the scenes, furnishing money and encouragement to indigenous groups.

In any event, whatever sense of national emergency—or despair—had moved Major Be and Mr. Chau to work with the CIA, it was easy to see what had moved the CIA to work with *them*, even assuming that they, too, might be "on probation." The ties that have come to light between the CIA and the intellectual community in the United States have surprising parallels in Vietnam—surprising, at least, to anyone who has not observed the gradual and typically modern fusion of intelligence with "intelligence." The CIA has been a promoter of various unorthodox experiments in South Vietnam, supplying not just the funds and some of the personnel, but the spark, the touch of genius allied to lunacy. The Green Berets, for instance, are referred to as a Spook outfit by our own government people in Saigon—usually with a wink. It is impossible to say how many of the books, not all bad, published about Vietnam have been financed, with or without the author's knowledge, by the CIA. They are backing the Khmer-Serai (Free Khmer), a right-wing movement against Prince Sihanouk and using the Special Forces—the Ho Chi Minh readers—near the Cambodian border to train Khmer-Serai troops. They have their own airline, Air America.

As in the U.S., the CIA in Vietnam prides itself on being more catholic in its patronage than overt government agencies. Congress, it is always argued in defense of secrecy, would be too stupid to vote appropriations for radical-sounding ventures, which is probably true. Congress might have bought Major Mai, strumming his guitar, but not Major Be. You would have to tone him down a bit for home consumption; what does he *mean,* Vietnamese society is completely corrupt? But beyond such practical considerations, the CIA has a real affinity with ex-leftists and pseudo-leftists of all stripes, as well as with the radical right. It *likes* intellectuals, which is natural, first because they are walking repositories of information, and second because the CIA sees itself as a lonely mastermind, the poet and unacknowledged legislator of the government. Finally, the CIA, collectively speaking, is an autodidact which never had time to get its Ph.D. and yearns to meet real, *motivated* political theorists and oddballs and have a *structured* conversation with them. The relentless resort to academic jargon about the war in Vietnam, on the part of half-educated spokesmen and commentators, doubtless reveals the CIA influence on people who may be unaware of it.

You never know whether someone you meet in Vietnam is a CIA agent or just a product of CIA thought. What about Sergeant Mulligan (not his real name), Boston College, B.A., Purdue University, M.A., did his Master's thesis on John C. Calhoun—"an original mind. The only original mind in American political thought. Jefferson stole everything from Locke and Adam Smith"? On the floor of his jeep is the *National Review* and *1964: The Fear Campaign Against Goldwater*. He despises the Arvin, who run instead of fighting (examples given); the only "friendly forces" he trusts in combat are the Khmer-Serai.

He is with "Special Services" but is on his way to dinner with the Green Berets (invitation extended): "the best talk in Saigon."

Or what about Colonel Corson (real name), a Marine tank commander in the hills above Da Nang, engaged in pacification? A graduate of the University of Chicago, studied with Korzybski, taught at a college in Florida, worked or served in China. Eleven thousand peasants are the material he has been given to mould. He defines the method he uses as Empirical Causality. He quotes Lenin: "Scratch a peasant, and you'll find a bourgeois." "Well, I'm scratching. And scratching." His young officers have made a painted scale model, like a crèche, in papier-mâché, of an ideal Vietnamese hamlet, which will probably really be built. Colonel Corson is ingenious. He has designed a large pigsty suited to local conditions and he is donating his Marine garbage to feed the peasants' pigs, solving two problems with one concise stroke. He has asked an engineer to design him a mill for the region, and the Marine engineer has designed the very latest thing. " 'Take it away,' I told him, 'and try to remember what a mill was like when you were a kid or when your father was a kid. Then build me that.' "

He is also cautious. He gave the peasants seeds and before going ahead with his hamlet program he waited to see whether they sold them on the black market. When they didn't, he proceeded. He is intelligent. He used Marine explosives to dynamite the fish in the river in order to show the peasants that there were bigger fish available than they were catching with their present nets. On the wall of his command post was a photograph of the dynamiting operation that seemed to be there mainly for his own pleasure. "I hope you're not planning to introduce fishing with dynamite to these people," I said. The answer was no. He had done it once, as a demonstration, and then given the fish to the peasants to sell on the market; with the profits, they were buying new and larger nets that would catch the bigger fish.

He is a cynic. To him, the profit motive is the sole incentive capable of spurring anybody to productive effort. "You wrote *The Group* to make money, didn't you?" When I answered no, the fact that it had made so much money had surprised me, he looked actually startled. "What do you write for, then?" In the center of the model hamlet, which his officers, like children at Christmas, had stayed up half the night to finish, was a large dollar sign, painted bronze. He gave a crooked smile. He was actually, or so he claimed, planning to erect it as a monument, seven feet high, in the hamlet. The young captain and the young lieutenant smiled. He was a man of whom it could be said, "He was worshipped by his officers." Partly because he amused them; he was witty and sardonic. And he had a sort of fantasy that did not chime badly with his brass tacks. In one corner of the model hamlet was a thatched apiary; one of the peasants was going to be transformed into a beekeeper. Bees and pigs and grains and big river fish—the colonel's georgic, though, had realism behind it. He was trying to wean the peasants away from the monoculture—rice—the French had saddled them with and which, with the rent system and government taxes, had turned them into paupers.

He did not want to be suspected of altruism. "I'm not doing any of this for the Vietnamese people. I'm doing it for *me*." He had challenged the Viet Cong to come into one of the hamlets, with a safe-conduct, at Christmas-time and debate him in the marketplace. They had refused the offer but then one night they had approached with loud-speakers, to broadcast against him to the people. " 'They just want you to make a buck,' the Viet Cong told them. And I said, 'Yeah. Yeah.' " There was a price, he was pleased to say, on the head of every one of his Civic Action people, which proved he was winning the argument. Empirical Causality was working. Or as he also called it, "the Charisma of Success."

He was not sparing of sarcasms for other American ideologists working in the field. He derided a study of a Vietnamese village made by an outfit of opinion-researchers that had worked for Kennedy in the 1960 election. "Two hundred thousand dollars was paid for that study, and they interviewed *six* Vietnamese." All the professorial research teams collecting and analyzing Vietnamese data—there are three, including RAND, on the scene—to the colonel, were softheaded or grafters or would-be thought-controllers or all three—a prejudiced opinion I shared, though I had not seen their studies, many of which are secret. I asked him what he thought of the Chieu Hoi program, to me one of the most odious features of the pacification drive. "We are just subsidizing traitors." The colonel agreed, though not for moral reasons. He thought it was stupid to try to make political converts of deserters. "Somebody dreamed that up in Arlington, Virginia. 'Open Arms!' If I want a man, I buy him." He did not seem to care for Johnson, whom he referred to as "Lyndon-Baby."

The thought that Colonel Corson was somewhat right-wing had been forcing itself into my mind, though I tried to shut the door on it. I drew a deep breath and asked him what he thought of Goldwater. The captain and the lieutenant at the neighboring desks stopped typing; they smiled quickly at each other. The colonel, musing, set down his beer glass. " 'In your heart you know he's stupid,' " he said with a grin. He had caught the direction of my question and told a story of throwing a one-armed (or one-legged) newspaperman down the stairs, back in Chicago. "He called me a Fascist and a Communist in the same breath." It was hard to find anybody on the American political horizon that Colonel Corson approved of, though he mentioned "a lady in Senator Jackson's office."

He believed in the $ as an instrument of Empirical Causality, but even in this profession of faith there was a note of saturnine self-mockery. The conversation became very confused when I remarked that most of his pacification ideas would work just as well in a socialist context. There was nothing specifically capitalist about feeding the Marines' garbage to the peasants' pigs. He tried to show me that the free market was crucial; Marx had not understood this. But I could not follow him because his language, suddenly, turned into an opaque forest of jargon substantives, and at that moment the unreality of the scene—the ironic colonel sitting like an unintelligible Socrates among his disciples with a model Vietnamese village on the table—struck me with wonder. He was good at gauging your thoughts. A few moments later, he said, as if idly, "There are no homosexuals in my battalion. If I find one, out he goes. The men that work for me have to like *girls*." And when I was complimenting him, mentally, on the peaceful idyl of his neat hut in the woods, he looked straight at me and said, as if to make sure there would be no misunderstanding: "I don't send anybody into Civic Action until they've been out and *killed.*" Colonel Corson was playing God and the Devil up there in the hills behind Da Nang. Unlike less reflective and less capable officers, he held the little country of Vietnam—where the people wore conical hats and lived in bamboo thickets—like a toy in his hand.

At the other end of the verbal spectrum, this Marine officer is possibly more of a revolutionist than Major Be. He was certainly more honest. But his tall bronze dollar sign is likely to remain his personal war monument—a symbol only, like Major Be's tractor. I doubted that Washington would ever let him build and unveil it. Despite his semantics, he is an *old-fashioned* free-enterpriser, being actually enterprising, for one thing, and out of sympathy with the principle of waste inherent in modern capitalism. And he exposed a little too frankly his contempt for the AID missionaries, for med-cap teams, and such sales gimmicks as the Chieu Hoi program, which other sources say is a brain child of the CIA. So that I would say no: the colonel, though sometimes scary and what he might call Machiavellian, is not a Spook.

The Open Arms Program is a typical instance of counterinsurgency thinking and has the earmarks of a CIA project: the CIA has a special rapport with the traitor (who, if he is not bought, is usually an intellectual), like the symbiosis between the policeman and the criminal. Of course it is not new to use traitors in wartime, but in the past their function has been restricted to opening the city gates by stealth, spying, and smuggling out information, sowing discontent among the population, as was tried in World War II by the modern means of radio-beaming. It is true, too, that deserters have often helped swing the balance in war, even when they simply went home—as many of the ARVN do now—and took no further part in the fighting. But the experiences of the Cold War and, later, of Cuba opened the minds of the Americans to the uses of the "defector"—a traitor and a deserter combined in one *politically conscious* person. The difference between a refugee or an exile and a defector is that the refugee or exile does not take on his status as a profession.

The idea of the Chieu Hoi program is not just to cause wide-scale desertions from the Viet Cong by loud-speakers broadcasting from planes and helicopters and by pamphlet drops, with the usual promises of money and good treatment—a natural enough proceeding in a civil war—but to turn every deserter into a defector by "re-educating" him in a camp. The Chieu Hoi centers are even more depressing than the refugee camps, although they are much less crowded and do not lack water and elementary sanitation. A Hoi Chanh or "returnee," once he turns himself in, becomes a prisoner condemned to a forty-five-to-sixty-day stretch for having "chosen freedom." He is finger-printed, interrogated ("The informing they do is on a purely voluntary basis," the American adviser emphasizes), indoctrinated, and finally released into society with a set of identity papers. In the Chieu Hoi camps I saw, which resembled old-fashioned reform schools, the inmates were roaming dully about the yard or simply lying listless on their bunks; one or two were writing letters. In theory, each defector receives vocational training (indeed a job is promised him by the loud-speakers), but the only evidence of this that was visible in one camp was a

Hoi Chanh sitting in a barber's chair having his hair cut by another Hoi Chanh, while, across the small dirty room, two tailor's apprentices were cutting out a pajama; in the other camp, it was Têt, and no one was doing anything, but there was no sign of equipment or tools to work with.

The Americans agree that the vocational program is not "rolling"; one explanation given is that the defectors are coming in so fast that they are overtaxing the facilities—another of the "problems of success." And the job prospects of the Hoi Chanh, trained or not, are bad. He re-enters society with the stigma of having been a Viet Cong, to which is added the stigma of treachery. The Americans at one time hoped to organize an army of defectors (on the Bay of Pigs model, no doubt), with colonels, captains, and other ranks; this, it was argued, would give the defectors "status." But the thought did not appeal to the Vietnamese army.

The most active part of the day in the Chieu Hoi camps is spent in indoctrination classes, where the defectors are supposedly decontaminated of VC ideology. Yet it seems that quite often the first they learn of the Viet Cong program is in these sessions, and many find it attractive—which may account for the regular one per cent that defect back at the end of the training period.

To join an Armed Propaganda Squadron probably represents the best job future for a Hoi Chanh. These are defectors organized into armed groups of thirty-six who travel about the country, as proselytizers, with the ARVN and the U.S. armed forces; when a hamlet is captured, their job is to question suspects. "Mean little kid, that one," said an American civilian, of one he found torturing a villager. That is their reputation, and it may be that those volunteering show a special ability for the work.

In February, the Chieu Hoi statistics were rising like a barometer. The return of these prodigal sons caused more exultation among higher-up Americans than the destruction of a Viet Cong rice cache or a successful bomb strike on the North. A victory for their leaflets and loud-speakers had come to mean more to them than a victory in the field. (All the time, as we now know, the ranks of the Viet Cong were mysteriously swelling, while infiltration from the North had diminished.) The Vietnamese themselves are not especially interested in the Chieu Hoi—they might prefer simply to shoot them on arrival—and the ordinary American soldiers, according to reporters, view them with disfavor. This badly damaged human material is a strange and shifty base on which to build a society. If fear or near-starvation brought them in (tuberculosis is frequent among defectors, an American source says), their change of allegiance is pitiable. If the promise of a job and money brought them in, it is sad. If our propaganda appeals brought them in, it is farcical.

According to official figures, 20,242 Chieu Hoi came over in 1966. It is hoped, at the very least, to double that in 1967. The political scientists, the OCO men, the AID men are watching, as they say, to see. What they do not see is the implications. If the pressures on the Viet Cong and its dependents increase, this means that mounting thousands of peasant guerrillas and part-time guerrillas will desert the Viet Cong and their villages to become jobless defectors; the target, presumably, would be total defection. No other formula for "integrating" the Viet Cong into Vietnamese life has been suggested.

The Open Arms Program and Revolutionary Development (which now, I notice, has quietly mutated into Rural Development—has Major Be been fired?) are the core, it is said with quiet satisfaction, of the U.S. and RVN pacification drive. The best that can be said of them is that, though totalitarian in ambition—isolate population cells and "re-educate" them for democracy—they are very inefficient.

The Chieu Hoi program, of course, is not dependent for its success on its absurd leaflets and broadcasts, but on military pressure, especially bombing, defoliation, crop-spraying, destruction of rice supplies, and what is known as "Resources Control." The stated object is to deprive the Viet Cong of food and other resources, including medical supplies and nurses: a native nurse suspected of treating the Viet Cong is liable to be executed, while an American nurse or an RVN nurse, if kidnapped or killed by a Viet Cong terror group, is, naturally, a civilian. What is not stated, though, is that the punitive measures taken to starve and weaken the Viet Cong punish more cruelly the non-combatants in VC territory, who, being non-combatants, cannot even interest the CIA as defectors. It has been estimated by a former Chieu Hoi who has made his way to Europe that a quarter of the population—peasants—will be killed or die of malnutrition or from lack of medical care.

To political scientists, however, the word "genocide" is quite unsuitable to describe what is happening. Genocide is *deliberate*. It is the same with bombs and mortars. If the Viet Cong plants a bomb in a theater, that is an atrocity, but if the Americans bomb a village that is "different." When you ask how it is different, the answer is that the VC action was deliberate, while the U.S. action was accidental. But in what way accidental if the fliers saw the village and could assume there were people in it and knew from experience that the bombs would go off? Well, the fliers were really aiming at the Viet Cong; if they hit some civilians, that was unintentional—it just happened. But it happens all the time, doesn't it? Yes, but each time it is an accident. In the American view, no area bombing implies premeditation of the results that follow, while every grenade hurled by a Viet Cong is launched in conformance with a *theory* and therefore possesses will and consciousness.

It is peculiar that the academic experts who have been studying guerrilla techniques, Communism, "wars of liberation" for nearly two decades have been unable to face the question of intention in this kind of warfare, where combatants and noncombatants are all but inseparable, while the means of killing and exterminating have been reaching a point close to perfection. Foreknowledge of the consequences of an action that is then performed generally argues the will to do it; if this occurs repeatedly, and the doer continues to protest that he did not will the consequences, that suggests an extreme and dangerous dissociation of the personality. Is that what is happening with the Americans in Vietnam, where words, as if "accidentally," have broken loose from their common meanings, where the Viet Cong guerrilla is pictured as a man utterly at one with his grenade, which fits him like an extension of his body, and the American, on the other hand, is pictured as completely sundered from his precision weaponry, as though he had no control over it, in the same way that Johnson, escalating, feigns to have no option in the war and to react, like an automat, to "moves" from Hanoi?

Solutions

"Well, what would you do?" Sooner or later, the critic of U.S. policy in Vietnam is faced with that question—a real crusher. Up to that point, he may have been winning the argument. His opponent may have conceded that it was a mistake to send American troops here in the first place, that there was no commitment under SEATO or any other "instrument" requiring it, that the war is horribly destructive, that pacification is not working, that Hanoi is not responding co-operatively to the bombing—in short, that everything that has been done up to the present instant has been wrong. But now resting comfortably on this mountain of errors, he looks down magnanimously on the critic and invites him to offer a solution. He is confident that the critic will be unable to come up with one. And in a sense he is right. If you say "Get Out"—the only sane answer—he pounces. "How?" And he sits back smiling. He has won. The tables are turned, and the critic is on the defensive. If he tries to outline a plan for rapid withdrawal, conscious that 464,000 troops, plus their civilian supporting services, cannot be pulled out overnight (and what about the "loyal" Vietnamese—should they be left behind or do we owe them an airlift to Taiwan?), the plan inevitably appears feeble and amateurish in comparison with the massed power and professionalism of the war actually being waged.

The fatal weakness in the thinking of most of Johnson's critics is not to perceive that that question is a booby trap. In general, the more eminent they are, the more alacrity they show in popping up with "positive recommendations for policy," "solutions," proposals for gradual and prudent disengagement, lest anybody think they are just carping and have no better alternatives of their own. Take the painful example of Arthur Schlesinger's *The Bitter Heritage*: "cogent, lucid, penetrating—tells us what really ought to be done about Vietnam" (John Gunther). It is cogent, lucid, penetrating *until* Schlesinger tells us what ought to be done in a wishful chapter entitled "The Middle Course," urging a political solution while insisting on the need to keep applying force (in moderation) to get it, the pursuit of negotiations while "tapering off" the bombing (no cease-fire on the ground, he warns—too dangerous), a promise to the Viet Cong of a "say" in the future of Vietnam but not, it is implied, too much of a say, reliance on Oriental "consensual procedures" or the precedent of Laos to solve any little difficulties in the way of a coalition government—a chapter that anyone who agrees with Schlesinger's negative arguments would like to snip out of the volume, working carefully with a razor blade so as to leave no traces before lending it to a less convinced friend. Presented with Schlesinger's formula for meeting the Communist "threat," the reader is likely to think that Johnson's formula is better.

The same sinking feeling was produced by Richard Goodwin in *The New Yorker*, by J. K. Galbraith's "moderate solution" (hailed by James Reston), by Senator Fulbright's eight-point program, and, sad to say, by the Fulbright hearings taken as a whole. What emerges, when all the talk is over, is that none of these people really opposes the war. Or not enough to stop thinking in terms of "solutions," all of which imply continuing the war by slightly different means until the Viet Cong or Hanoi (Schlesinger holds out the exciting possibility of an "exploitable split" between the Viet Cong and Hanoi) is ready to make peace.

Even a man like George Kennan, who evidently believes the war to be wrong and testified impressively against our policy before the Fulbright Committee, did not have an inner attorney to warn him to rest his case there. Instead, pressed by bullish senators to say what he would do in the President's place (never mind what he would have *done*), Kennan fell back on the enclave strategy, making an easy target for the military, who can demonstrate without trouble how enclaves failed the French in *their* war, how Tito's Partisans knew they had won when they finally maneuvered the Nazis into coastal enclaves, how in fact the last place you want to be when faced with guerrillas is holed up in an enclave. And Kennan himself must have known that he had lost a round in the fight for peace when he allowed himself to be cornered into offering inconsequent armchair recommendations, in the midst of the hostile terrain, bristling with alert TV aerials, of U.S. popular feeling.

These are the errors of an opposition that wants to be statesmanlike and responsible, in contrast to the "irresponsible" opposition that is burning its draft card or refusing to pay taxes. To make sure that it can be told apart from these undesirables, it behaves on occasion like a troop of Eagle Scouts. Think of the ludicrous message sent to North Vietnam by sixteen Congressional doves—an appeal to Ho to understand that they are

a) an unrepresentative minority and b) loyal Americans whose speeches were not meant to be overheard and "misinterpreted" by Hanoi.

Or it can assume the voice of Johnson. A recent New York *Post* editorial sternly criticized the Ky government's suspension of free speech (guaranteed by the new Constitution) and then continued: "We cannot heed the counsel of timid or misguided persons and withdraw. We dare not shrink from the duty democracy demands." The truth is, the *Post* is too cowardly to call for withdrawal. For the respectable opposition, unilateral withdrawal has become steadily more unthinkable as United States intervention has widened. It was perfectly thinkable before 1961. It was even thinkable for Bobby Kennedy as late as September 1963, at a meeting of the National Security Council, when he asked whether *now* might be the time to get out. It is still thinkable, though not by the Kennedy men, who, out of power, dare not reason as they might have in the privacy of a president's councils.

We could still, if we wished, take "French leave" of Vietnam, and *how* this should be done ought not to be the concern of those who oppose our presence there. When the French schoolteachers and intellectuals of the Committee of 121 insisted that France get out of Algeria, they did not supply De Gaulle with a ten-point program telling him how to do it. That was De Gaulle's business. He was responsible, not they. As intellectuals, they confronted their government with an unequivocal moral demand, and far from identifying themselves with that government and thinking helpfully on its behalf, they disassociated themselves from it totally so long as it continued to make war in Algeria. The administrative problems of winding up the war were left to those who had been waging it, just as the political problem of reconciling the French electorate to a defeat was left in the hands of De Gaulle, a politician by profession.

Our pamphleteers and polemicists, if they were resolute, would behave in the same way. Not: "We see your dilemma, Mr. President. It won't be easy to stop this war, but here are a few ideas." The country needs to understand that the war is wrong, and the sole job of the opposition should be to enforce that understanding and to turn it, whenever possible, into the language of action. It is clear that U.S. senators and former ambassadors are not going to sit in at the Pentagon or hurl themselves at troop trains; nobody expects that of them and nobody seriously expects elected or appointed officials to practice tax refusal. But one *could* expect practical support for the young people who are resisting the draft from a few courageous officeholders and from private figures with a genuine sense of public responsibility.

Instead of hoping to avoid identification with unruly picketers and other actionists, Americans who are serious in opposing the war should be refusing to identify themselves with the U.S. government, even a putative government that would change to a defensive "posture" and prepare, as they say, to sit the war out. The question is simple: Do I disapprove *more* of the sign that picket is carrying—and the beard he is wearing—or of the Vietnamese war? To judge by introspection, the answer is not pretty. For the middle-class, middle-aged "protestor," the war in Vietnam is easier to take than a sign that says "JOHNSON MURDERER."

The war does not threaten our immediate well-being. It does not touch us in the consumer-habits that have given us literally our shape. Casualty figures, still low, seldom strike home outside rural and low-income groups—the silent part of society. The absence of sacrifices has had its effect on the opposition, which feels no need, on the whole, to turn away from its habitual standards and practices—what for? We have not withdrawn our sympathy from American power and from the way of life that is tied to it—a connection that is more evident to a low-grade G.I. in Vietnam than to most American intellectuals.

A sympathy, sneaking or otherwise, for American power is weakening the opposition's case against Johnson. He acts as if he had a mournful obligation to go on with the war unless and until somebody finds him an honorable exit from it. There is no honorable exit from a shameful course of action, though there may be a lucky escape. But the mirage of an honorable exit—a "middle road"—remains the deceptive premise of the liberal opposition, which urges the mistrustful President to attempt it on a pure trial-and-error basis; you never know, it may work.

For example, "Stop the bombing to get negotiations"—meaning the bombing of the North; strangely, nothing is said about the much worse bombing of the South. But in reality no one knows, unless it is Ho Chi Minh, whether a cessation of bombing would bring negotiations or not and, if it did, what the terms of Ho would be. Stop it for six months and see, suggests Bobby Kennedy. "Don't pin it down. Be vague," others say. But how does this differ, except in duration, from one of Johnson's famous bombing pauses, which failed, so he claimed, to produce any response? Moreover, if stopping the bombing is only a trick or maneuver to get negotiations (that is, to see the enemy's cards), then Rusk and Joseph Alsop have equal rights to argue that talk of negotiations, put about by the friends of Hanoi, is only a trick to stop the bombing and give the North a chance to rebuild. And what if the bombing stops and Hanoi does come to the conference table or comes with intransigent terms? Then the opposition, it would seem, is bound to agree to more and perhaps bigger bombing. Advocates of a failed hypothesis in wartime can only fall silent and listen to Big Brother.

To demand a halt to the bombing unconditionally, without qualifications, is quite another matter. The citizen who makes that demand cannot be "proved" wrong by subsequent developments, *e.g.*, the obduracy of Hanoi or an increase in infiltration. Either it is *morally* wrong for the United States to bomb a small and virtually defenseless country or it is not, and a student picketing the Pentagon is just as great an expert in that realm, to say the least, as Dean Rusk or Joseph Alsop. Surely, in fact, the student who *demands* that the bombing stop speaks with a greater authority than the professor who *urges* it.

Not being a military specialist, I cannot plot the logistics of withdrawing 464,000 American boys from Vietnam, but I know that it can be done, if necessary, and Johnson knows it too. *Everybody* knows it. A defeat in battle on the order of Dien Bien Phu, if it happened, could provide Johnson's generals with the opportunity to plan and execute a retreat. That is their job, and Johnson might even snatch honor from it. Look at Churchill and the heroic exploit of Dunkirk, which did not depend on prior negotiations with Hitler. But we cannot wait for a major defeat in battle to cover Johnson's withdrawal with honor or even to save his face for him. Nor can we wait for a Soviet or a Chinese intervention, which might have the same effect (if not a quite different one) by precipitating a Cuban-style confrontation; the war could then terminate in a withdrawal of the big powers, leaving a wrecked Vietnam to the Vietnamese. That, no doubt, would be a "solution" acceptable to the men in power.

In politics, it seems, retreat is honorable if dictated by military considerations and shameful if even *suggested* for ethical reasons—as though, by some law of inertia, force could only yield to superior force or to some natural obstacle, such as unsuitable terrain or "General Winter," whom Napoleon met in Russia. Thus the immense American superiority of arms *in itself* becomes an argument for staying in Vietnam; indeed, at this point, the only argument. The more troops and matériel committed to Vietnam, the more retreat appears to be cut off—not by an enemy, but by our own numbers. To call for withdrawal in the face of that commitment (the only real one we have made to Vietnam) is to seem to argue not against a policy, but against *facts*, which by their very nature are unanswerable. In private, a U.S. spokesman may agree that the Americans cannot win in Vietnam. "But they can't lose either," he adds with a satisfied nod. Critics of U.S. policy, when they go to Vietnam, are expected to be convinced by the fact of 464,000 troops, once it sinks in; and indeed what can you say to it? Johnson's retort to his opponents has been to tersely add *more* facts, in the shape of men and arms. Their utility is not just to overwhelm the Viet Cong by sheer force of numbers, but to overwhelm domestic disbelief; if they cannot stop the VC, they can stop any talk of unilateral withdrawal. Under these circumstances, the idea that he subtract a few facts—de-escalation—is rejected by Johnson as illogical. The logic of numbers is the only one that convinces him of the rightness of the course he is bent on.

Meanwhile, the generals are sure they could win the war if they could only bomb the port of Haiphong and the Ho Chi Minh trail in Laos. They blame politics for their failure to win it, and by politics is meant the existence of counter-forces in the theater: China, Russia, the Pathet Lao, and simply people, civilians, a weak counter-force, but still an obstacle to total warfare under present conditions. It used to be said that the balance of terror would give rise to a series of limited wars. Up to now, this has been true, so far as geographical scale goes, but the abstention from the use of atomic arms, in Vietnam, has not exactly worked to moderate the war.

On the contrary, the military establishment, deprived for the time being of tactical atomic weapons (toys being kept in the closet) and held back from bombing the port of Haiphong and the Ho Chi Minh trail, has compensated for these limitations by developing other weapons and devices to the limit: antipersonnel bombs; a new, more adhesive napalm; a twenty-pound gadget, the E-63 manpack personnel detector, made by General Electric, replacing British-trained bloodhounds, to sniff out Viet Cong; a battery-powered blower that raises the temperature in a VC tunnel network to 1000 degrees Fahrenheit (loud-speakers, naturally, exhort the Viet Cong in the tunnels to surrender); improved tear gases; improved defoliants. The classic resistance offered by climate and terrain to armies of men, one of the ancient limitations on warfare, will doubtless be all but eliminated as new applications for patents pour into the U.S. Patent Office. The jungle will be leafless and creeperless, and the mangrove swamps dried out; the weather will be controlled, making bombing possible on a 365-day-a-year basis, exclusive of Buddha's birthday,

Christmas, and Têt. The diseases of the jungle and tropical climates are already pretty well confined to the native population, thanks to pills and immunization. In other words, for an advanced nation, practically no obstacles remain to the exercise of force except "politics."

U.S. technology is bent on leaving nothing to chance in the Vietnamese struggle, on taking the risk out of war (for ourselves, of course, while increasing the risk for the enemy). Whatever cannot be controlled scientifically—shifts of wind, rain—is bypassed by radar and electronics. Troop performance is fairly well guaranteed by the Selective Service system and by rotation; the "human element," represented by the Arvin, prone to desert or panic, is despised and feared. And if chance can be reduced to a minimum by the "miracle" of American technology, there is only one reality-check on American *hubris*: the danger of Chinese or Russian intervention, which computers in the Pentagon are steadily calculating, to take the risk out of *that*.

Yet the peculiar fact is that this has been a war of incredible blunders, on the American side; you never hear of blunders, though there must be some, on the part of the Viet Cong. Leaving aside the succession of political blunders, starting with the great Diem gamble and going right up to the Ky gamble (the current embarrassment of U.S. officials), there has been a startling number of military blunders: government villages bombed, Cambodian villages bombed, a Strategic Hamlet gunned by a U.S. helicopter on the day before the ambassador's scheduled visit, U.S. troops bombed and shelled by their own aircraft and artillery, "Friendlies" bombed and shelled, a Russian ship bombed in Haiphong harbor, overflights into China.

In the case of North Vietnam, blunder must be a misnomer for what has been done with regularity to villages, churches, hospitals, a model leper colony, schools. American opinion refuses to hear of a "deliberate bombing pattern" in North Vietnam, though there is plenty of testimony and photographic evidence of the destruction of populated centers. The administration insists that we are bombing military targets only, though it has finally conceded, after too many had been found, that we were using antipersonnel bombs in the North, without specifying how these inventions, designed to fragment a soft human body, were effective against bridges, power plants, and railway yards. Yet even those who are unconvinced by the administration's regularly issued denials prefer to think that what is happening is the result of human or mechanical error—a possibility categorically excluded by the U.S. Navy.

On the nuclear carrier *Enterprise*, a squadron of Intruder pilots in their air-conditioned ready room assured journalists, myself included, that under no circumstances did they hit anything in the North but military targets. How did they know? Because they only bombed targets assigned to them, which had been carefully selected with the aid of computers working on aerial photographs. Besides, post-raid reconnaissance recorded on film the "impact" of every delivery; there was no chance of error. Did it never happen that, returning from a mission and having failed for some reason—flak or whatever—to reach their assigned targets, they jettisoned their bomb load on the countryside? Never. Always into the sea. What about those accounts of devastated villages and hamlets? Impossible. "Our aerial photographs would show it." You could not shake their placid, stolid, almost uninterested conviction. Yet somebody's cameras were lying. Those of the journalists and other witnesses who bring back ordinary photographs they have snapped in the North or the unmanned cameras of the U.S. Navy?

Their faith in technology had put these men, in their own eyes, above suspicion. They would as soon have suspected the totals of an adding machine. Was it conceivable that in flying they kept their attention glued to their instrument panels and their radar screen, watching out for MIGs and SAMs, no more interested in what was *below* them, in both senses, than they were in our questions?

The same faith in technology commands the administration to go on with the war, in defiance of any evidence of failure, bringing to bear American inventiveness, not only in the field of weaponry, but also in the field of propaganda—loud-speakers, broadcasts from the air, cunning messages inserted literally between the lines of ornamented New Year's calendars distributed free to the people—"We don't make it too obvious." The next step in this field would be subliminal suggestion, psychedelic bombardments in light and color to be pioneered by General Electric, free "trips" offered to the population by the Special Forces, with CIA backing —the regular Army would disapprove.

"Politics" gets in the way of technology. If the world could be cleansed of politics, including South Vietnamese politicians, victory might be in sight. Politics, domestic and international, is evidently the only deterrent recognized by the Americans to an all-out onslaught on the Vietnamese nation; it is the replacement of the inner voice of conscience, which nobody but a few draft-resisters can hear. Johnson, who keeps acting as if he were bowing to necessity, looks to "politics"—*i.e.*, Hanoi—to release him, the prisoner of circumstance. He invites his enemy and his critics to "show him the way out." At the same time he insists that "the door is always open," which means, if anything, that the portals of peace will swing wide at the bidding of Ho Chi Minh but remain locked to *him*, beating and signaling from the inside. What he appears to be saying is that Ho Chi Minh is free whereas he and his advisers are not.

This hypocritical performance may, like most play-acting, have a certain psychological truth. Johnson and his advisers, like all Americans, are the conditioned subjects of the free-enterprise system, which despite some controls and government manipulation, appears to function automatically, requiring no consent on the part of those involved in it. A sense of compulsion, dictated by the laws of the market, permeates every nerve of the national life. Industry, for example, has been "compelled" to automate by the law of cost-cutting, which works in "free" capitalism with the same force as a theorem in geometry. And the necessity to automate is accepted throughout society without any question. The human damage involved, if seen close up, may elicit a sigh, as when a co-operative apartment building fires its old Negro elevator operators ("Been with us twenty years") to put in self-service: "We had to, you see. It was cheaper." Or ask a successful author why he has changed from his old publisher, who was virtually his parent, to a new mass-market one. "I had to," he explains, simply. "They offered me more money."

A feeling of having no choice is becoming more and more widespread in American life, and particularly among successful people, who supposedly are free beings. On a concrete plane, the lack of choice is often a depressing reality. In national election years, you are free to choose between Johnson and Goldwater or Johnson and Romney or Reagan, which is the same as choosing between a Chevrolet and a Ford—there is a marginal difference in styling. Just as in American hotel rooms you can decide whether or not to turn on the air conditioner (that is *your* business), but you cannot open the window.

It is natural that in such a system the idea of freedom is associated with escape, whether through trips or "trips," rather than with the exercise of one's ordinary faculties. And at the same time one's feeling of imprisonment is joined to a conviction of innocence. Johnson, perhaps genuinely, would like to get out of his "commitment" to the war in Vietnam, and the more deeply he involves himself in it, the more abused and innocent he feels, and the less he is inclined to take any steps to release *himself*, for to do so would be to confess that he is culpable or—the same thing—that he has been free at any time to do what he would now be doing.

Those of Johnson's critics who, like Senator Fulbright, repudiate the thought of a "disorderly" retreat by implication favor an orderly retreat, with the panoply of negotiations, guarantees, and so on. *I.e.*, a retreat assisted and facilitated by Hanoi. But that choice, very likely, is no longer open, thanks to Johnson himself. He would be very lucky, at this point, to get negotiations at the mere cost to him of ending the bombing of the North—a cost that to Ho or any rational person seems derisory, since, as our military spokesmen have complained, there are no targets in North Vietnam left to destroy, except the port of Haiphong, which Johnson, for his own reasons and not to please Ho, has spared up to now. Indeed, to have something of value to offer short of troop withdrawal, Johnson's peculiar logic would lead him to *start* bombing the port of Haiphong in order to *stop* bombing it—exactly the chain of reasoning that sent our planes north back in February 1965, and has kept them pounding ever since.

The opposition's best hopes for an orderly retreat rest on the South Vietnamese, just as, probably, the administration's fears do. The notion that the elections this September *might* put in a government that could negotiate a separate peace with the NLF is once again reviving; some people are daring to bank on the return of General Minh as a coalition candidate. *If* he is permitted to return and if *he* is elected, with the support of the radical Buddhists and liberal groups in the Constitutional Assembly, that would allow the Americans to leave by invitation—a very attractive prospect. And were they to decline the invitation and try to depose him (as in effect they did once before, considering him too "leftish"), they might have a double civil war on their hands, a more serious repetition of what happened in the spring of 1966. In either case, the Vietnamese elections could be a turning point. Or, failing that, the American elections of 1968. The opposition prays for the nomination of a Romney or a Percy, who *might* beat Johnson and *might* end the war, as Eisenhower did in Korea. And it dreads the nomination of a Nixon or a Reagan, which would "compel" it to vote again for Johnson—a perfect illustration of American consumer choice.

These are all hopes for a Redeemer who will come from the *outside* to save us from our own actions: an Asian general, a Republican who does not fit into the party program or picture. In the same way, Johnson may be hoping for a Redeemer in the form of Kosygin to get him to the peace table. Or he may have a more far-reaching design: the eventual occupation of the North and the establishment of U.S. bases next to the Chinese border. Yet if such a design exists, it must be in the *back* of the administration's mind and be, itself, more a cunning hope than a businesslike calculation, a thought held in the pending file and marked "Cosmic."

Actually, so far as is known, Johnson has no program for ending the war in the South. Asked what *he* would do, he, too, no doubt would be reduced to head-scratching. He has given a promise to withdraw American troops as soon as hostilities are over—a promise that evidently cannot be kept. The consequences of bilateral withdrawal would be nearly as "disastrous" as the consequences of unilateral withdrawal: the return of the Viet Cong. The Vietnamese know this, which makes them uncertain what to fear most. A new man in the White House who might decide to keep it? Or permanent colonial status?

"The Vietnamese must choose for themselves," the Americans repeat, having done their best to deprive them of the power of choice during thirteen years of American military assistance that slowly turned into a full-scale American invasion—there is no other word for it. The Americans pretend that this was somehow forced on them; in reality, it was forced on the Vietnamese, as is clear from the low morale of their troops. "They just don't want to fight," American officers say with an air of puzzlement. If the Vietnamese want to be rid of the Americans, they must turn toward the NLF—a hard decision for some French-educated idealists, who, despite their experience with the American brand as an export product, still have hopes of democracy. Yet the brutality of the war is reconciling certain middle-class Saigon groups to making discreet overtures toward their class enemy; meanwhile, in the field, the Viet Cong forces have been increasing—which our spokesmen ascribe to "better recruiting methods." In their turn, Americans concerned for the future of the Republic, rather than for the future of American power, are reduced to hoping that the Viet Cong can hold out in the face of the overwhelming *facts* marshaled against it—as though its often primitive and homemade weapons possessed a moral force of resistance denied to members of the Great Society.

The uselessness of our free institutions, pleasurable in themselves, to interpose any check on a war of this character, opposed, though not enough, by most so-called thinking persons, suggests that freedom in the United States is no longer a political value and is seen simply as the right to self-expression, as in the dance, psychodrama, be-ins, kinky sex, or baking ceramics. The truth is, only a minority is *interested* in the war in Vietnam, and debate about the subject is treated as a minority pastime, looked on by the majority with more or less tolerance. "The country can afford it," is the attitude. Or: "It's a free country," which has come to mean "I've got mine, Jack. Everybody to his taste." A little less tolerance might harden the opposition. If the opposition wants to make itself felt politically, it ought to be acting so as to provoke intolerance. It is hurt because the administration ignores it. There are various ways of obliging the administration—and more importantly the country—to take notice: some extremely radical, like the bonze's way of self-immolation; some less so, ranging from tax refusal through the operation of underground railroads for protesting draftees, down to simple boycotts of key war industries; nobody who is against the war should be receiving dividends from the manufacture of napalm, for instance, which is calling to be outlawed.

Since the Revolution, this country has had no experience of foreign occupation and consequently of resistance movements; in that field, it lacks inspiration and inventiveness and is readily discouraged. But the professors and students who lost heart when the teach-ins failed to change U.S. policy might study the example of the Abolitionists—the nearest thing to a resistance movement the Republic has had. Obviously no single plan of action can stop the war in Vietnam, and maybe a hundred plans concerted could not stop it. But if it can be stopped, it will be through initiatives taken by persons or groups of persons (whether they be Johnson or Ho or a Republican president or Big Minh or the readers of this pamphlet) and not through cooked-up "solutions" handed to somebody else to act on, like inter-office memoranda. The "hard thinking" about this war needs to begin at home, with the critic asking himself what *he* can do against it, modestly or grandly, with friends or alone. From each according to his abilities, but to be in the town jail, as Thoreau knew, can relieve any sense of imaginary imprisonment.